# SUCCESSFULLY LAUNCHING A HEDGE FUND IN EUROPE

Edited By

*SIMON KERR*

PUBLISHED BY

**HEDGE FUND INSIGHT**

# Published by

# Hedge Fund Insight

# www.hedgefundinsight.org

Cover Design by Eleanor Russell Jones

ISBN: 978-0-9956475-0-3

# INTRODUCTION

It has been some time since a book was published to help new hedge fund managers get launched in Europe. In the decade since the last one a lot has changed in the financial world and specifically in the hedge fund industry.

This book is intended to provide a road map to setting up a hedge fund in Europe in this more challenging operating environment. The processes that need to take place are described, and the key decisions that have to be made are identified here.

If you enjoyed this book, found it useful or otherwise then please post a short review on Amazon.

# TABLE OF CONTENTS

# ACKNOWLEDGEMENTS

Thanks go to the contributors for their patience and commitment to the project, in particular to the pseudonymous contributor of Chapter 10, hedge fund COO "George Alexander".

Thanks also to Stuart MacDonald of Bride Valley Partners for suggestions and copy reading.

It is appreciated that Preqin generated data specifically for this book.

Thank you Eleanor Russell Jones for hitting inspiration point with the cover.

# CHAPTER 1. THE LAUNCH ENVIRONMENT

## By Simon Kerr

## About the author

*Simon Kerr is the Publisher of Hedge Fund Insight. He is an experienced analyst and commentator on both financial markets and hedge funds. He was a first quartile money manager running portfolios for institutional investors and was a recognised authority in the use of derivatives. He has risk management expertise across fund formats and asset classes. He has been in the hedge fund industry since 1998 and has experience of many aspects: he has acted as a consultant, portfolio manager, fund director, marketer and COO in the hedge fund business. Simon has been a high-scoring trainer for Henley Business School since 2012. His first book on hedge funds was published by Informa in 1999.*

## About Hedge Fund Insight

Hedge Fund Insight, an internet-only media title and events company. The website is a publisher/curator of commentary and analysis of the hedge fund industry. It carries podcasts and videos, as well as commissioned, written features. Articles are always supported by graphics, and can be brief in the "Shorts & Humour" section, or as substantial as a full 3,000 word profile article. The longest item on HFI is 7,000 words long. Hedge Fund Insight was launched in 2012 and ran its first event in November of 2015.

# THE INDUSTRY CONTEXT

The hedge fund industry is in one of its pause phases as this book is published. Aggregate industry assets have not grown over the last year. Flows into hedge funds in 2016 were mildly positive early in the year, but there were net redemptions thereafter. For the first time in several years the biggest managers of hedge funds have not taken market share. 59% of the hedge fund management groups in a recent Pensions & Investments survey reported a decline in assets they managed worldwide in hedge funds compared with the year-earlier period, when 70% reported asset growth.

It has never been easy to launch a hedge fund – and, at the least, the challenges of doing it have varied through time. The first peak of the modern industry came pre-Credit Crunch. In 2008 a record of nearly 1,200 new hedge funds came to market. The whole universe consisted of 10,200 hedge funds at that time.

Around 2007-8 most of the flows into single manager hedge funds were via funds of hedge funds. This phenomenon was good for start-up and new managers as funds of funds through their multi-manager vehicles or dedicated seeding funds had a variety of business models. This enabled a range of types of start-up funds/management companies to secure the necessary backing.

The hedge fund industry post-Madoff, and post-liquidity crunch has been very different from before. The whole industry was in hunker-down mode in 2009 after HNWI capital had flooded out of hedge funds (when it could get through the gates). The first flows back in to the industry came in the Autumn of 2009. And those inflows were almost exclusively institutional. Then and for some time after, although flows in aggregate were positive they were concentrated among the brand name hedge fund management groups, that is amongst the largest global managers.

The environment for new and emerging managers only improved well after that for the largest well-established hedge fund managers, but it did improve as the sources of industry flows diversified. It has been estimated that capital for seeding in 2016 is half of the level of capital available in 2008. Eventually (from 2011 onwards) private wealth has come back to investing in hedge funds through family offices and private banks. As a corollary, family offices are once again backers of early stage managers.

## FUNDS OF HEDGE FUNDS

The commercial environment for funds of hedge fund groups is hugely different post-Madoff. Fee pressures are constant and costs have gone up for remaining in the business. There are less assets under management at funds of hedge funds and fewer funds of funds groups engaged in investing than there were pre-2009. And these are both medium-to-long term trends.

As it has gone ex-growth, the sector has been consolidating ever since Madoff, and within this trend there are relatively few winners and many losers. The exceptions are the consolidators in the sector, those taking market share and the few new entrants.

Whereas up to 2008 just about every fund of funds would say they invested in new hedge funds (and it was true), most funds of funds post-Madoff will respond to surveys saying they are prepared to back new funds, but won't. Last year only 18% of funds of funds that were respondents to an InvestHedge survey said they were not currently investing in emerging managers. 97% of funds of funds said they were prepared to be Day One investors. Better yet, 50% of the funds of funds in that survey had dedicated emerging manager product and one in three of the balance were considering having such a product.

The significance of the dedicated product for emerging managers is that there is an inference of turnover – which creates openings for new managers. The funds of emerging managers may succeed (in which case they graduate to the flagship and mainstream portfolios of funds), they may produce typical returns (in which case they may be funded in a fund of funds for a maximum period of time, say 2 or 3 years), or the funds may fail in performance terms – in which case the holdings will be sold and capital is available to invest elsewhere. Whatever the performance outcome, per se there has to be turnover in an emerging manager fund. The exception to this is where there is a seeding deal – where some of the business economics of the emerging manager are owned by the fund of funds business.

A third source of capital for start-ups, after family offices and funds of hedge funds, is platforms and, to a limited extent, accelerators. The increased institutionalisation and regulation of the hedge fund industry has meant that the embedded costs of a start-up and the ongoing expenses of running the business are both significantly higher now than pre-Credit Crunch. A consequence has been a decline in independently-funded launches. At a Bloomberg hedge fund start up conference held in London recently a speaker said that 80% of hedge fund launches in Europe were done by groups that had cut a deal with a backer, or were hosted by another hedge fund-associated business. It has got to the point that it is unusual in Europe for a hedge fund management company founder to be taking all the entrepreneurial risk of starting a new business.

## INVESTOR DEMAND FOR EUROPEAN FUNDS OR GOOD FUNDS?

Investor demand for hedge funds managed from Europe is subject to the same factors as for funds managed from anywhere else. The number one criterion is performance. It has been so historically and always will be. The investment strategy undertaken is, of course, important to investors. For the most part the investment strategy and performance are much more important than where the manager is based. Investors in hedge funds will select the best manager for the investment strategy slot they have in mind in their portfolio at the point of search. Overwhelmingly a rational long-list then short-list is put together. Mostly the search is not a function of where the manager is based, but there are behavioural biases amongst investors in hedge funds.

Whilst even very large investors say that they are prepared to invest in the very best (or most suitable) managers wherever they are based, that is not borne out by the facts. There are research budgets for investors in hedge funds, and it is more productive for consultants or the heads of research at a fund of funds to go to the Tri-state area and London to find an additional hedge fund than to go elsewhere. In the extreme cases perfectly good managers based in New Zealand, Australia, South Africa and Israel have had a hard time raising cross-border capital for their offshore funds.

These biases are also at play in less extreme cases. In the context of the United States it can be more difficult for a manager based in Florida or Minnesota to raise capital than a manager based in San Francisco, Chicago or Westchester. In Europe a manager based in Paris, like CTA Capital Fund Management, should not struggle for cross-border capital on account of its location. But there are examples of hedge fund managers who have had to move their physical location, if not their tax domicile or nominal HQ, to make it easier for investors to visit them (or to get regulatory approval from a more understanding regulator).

To be more localised, since three-quarters of Europe's hedge funds are in London, the same arguments apply to office location within London. Of course there are hedge funds located outside London's M25 – indeed being based in Cambridge has not noticeably held back Cantab Capital – but I would observe that the management of the funds I have known based in Islington, Hammersmith and Wimbledon would probably not base themselves outside of the City or West End if starting over in London today.

The most logical circumstance for looking for a European-based manager would be when looking for a manager that specialises in managing European assets. But that is not to say that European-based managers are expected by investors to specialise in Europe investment strategies. It is as likely that a European-based manager would specialise in Asian equities, quantitative methods or oil-rig-financing as investing in European stocks or bonds. To return to where we started with investor demand, the most important thing to attract investor interest is the fund's performance (historic and prospective). To the extent that the return series of a European-based manager is superior in scale, lack of correlation or lesser variance to hedge fund managers based anywhere else then that will attract investor interest.

As a neophyte hedge fund manager you should be aware then that you are competing for capital on a global basis. To succeed commercially you need to be perceived to be better than managers in the same investment strategy, wherever they are based. Even when an investment strategy is unusual and true comparisons are difficult, that will not stop investors in hedge funds and their advisors attempting to put a fund in a box or style grouping.

# EUROPE ACTIVE IN LAUNCHES AND LIQUIDATIONS IN 2016

There are a lot of hedge funds already in existence. According to Hedge Fund Research (HFR) at the end of 3Q 2016, the total number of active single-manager hedge funds was 8,349, down from the 3Q 2015 record of 8,566. Total capital under management in the industry fell from over $3 trillion to $2.97 trillion over the same period. "The environment for new hedge funds continues to be extremely competitive with discriminating investors exhibiting low tolerance for under performance, resulting in an elevated number of liquidations," observed Kenneth J. Heinz, President of HFR last year.

As a global trend fund launches are becoming less frequent. A total of 576 funds were launched in the first three quarters of 2016, according to HFR - a decline of over 200 from the 785 launches over the same period the previous year. Launches, along with everything else in the hedge fund industry, tend to be dominated by North American activity. Over 700 new hedge funds were launched by American managers last year, compared with 191 by European-based managers. But even in the United States, the home of most hedge fund managers and the source of most of the capital going into hedge funds in the last five years, the amount of capital committed to new hedge funds was down 41% in the first half of the year. The global trend is fewer launches and smaller launches.

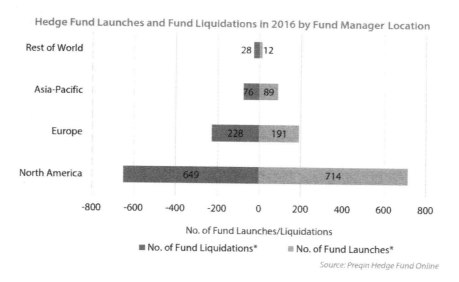

Hedge Fund Launches and Fund Liquidations in 2016 by Fund Manager Location

Source: Preqin Hedge Fund Online

The increasingly tough operating environment for hedge funds is reflected in the net change in the number of hedge funds in Europe – that is, new funds launching less funds closing in each period.

## Net Change in Number European Hedge Funds By Year

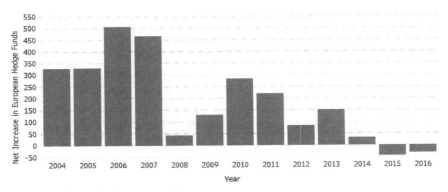

Source: Eurekahedge 2016 data as of Sept. 21

Since hedge fund management companies started being formed in Europe in the mid-to-late 1990's the number of funds grew each year, even through the Credit Crunch. That growth by number of funds has reversed in the last two years. In 2015 and 2016 more hedge funds in Europe were liquidated than were launched.

Within Europe, the UK has long been the home of most of Europe's hedge fund management companies. In terms of assets the UK represents over 70% of the Europe's hedge funds. So with a well-trodden path and established, high-quality service providers it is unsurprising that the UK also has the largest share of hedge fund launches. At the end of July 2016 data from Preqin showed the level of UK launch activity to be down slightly year-on-year, and that rate of decline was less than the rest of Europe.

After the UK the countries with the next highest hedge fund launch activity are Switzerland and France, both long-standing centres of asset management. As per the UK, activity has trended down over the last five years, though in both Continental countries to a greater extent. Whilst the number of launches by UK-based managers are down by a third in the medium term, in Switzerland and France new launches are down by two-thirds over the last five years.

8

## Hedge Fund Launches in Europe by Country

| Year | UK | Sweden | Switz-erland | France | Germany | Luxem-bourg | Europe |
|---|---|---|---|---|---|---|---|
| 2011 | 193 | 4 | 33 | 36 | 11 | 11 | 326 |
| 2012 | 167 | 11 | 38 | 41 | 10 | 9 | 327 |
| 2013 | 161 | 6 | 39 | 25 | 11 | 9 | 284 |
| 2014 | 141 | 6 | 38 | 23 | 4 | 12 | 267 |
| 2015 | 140 | 7 | 11 | 13 | 7 | 5 | 205 |
| 2016 YTD | 63 | 9 | 7 | 5 | 2 | 2 | 98 |

Source: Preqin    Data to End July 2016

A bright spot in the area of hedge fund launches is alternative UCITS funds. According to data carried in HFMWeek, launches of alternative UCITS have actually increased in the first half of last year – by as much as 25%, even as hedge fund start-up activity has fallen globally. There were 130 alternative UCITS launches in the first six months of 2016, compared to 104 a year earlier. You can get input on whether the UCITS format is the right one for your hedge fund elsewhere in this book.

# CHAPTER 2. MANAGING THE LAUNCH PROJECT

By Peter Northcott of KB Associates

## About the author

*Peter Northcott works for KB Associates as an Operational Consultant based in London. His principal practice areas are working with start-up hedge fund managers as a "Virtual COO" and advising established managers as to how to prepare for investor operational due diligence. He also represents KB Associates more broadly in the London market.*

*Peter has worked in the financial services industry since 1989. He has expertise as a hedge fund COO, including managing several launches, in operational due diligence and in change management.*

*Prior to joining KB Associates, Peter was a COO at the hedge fund managers Mako Global Investors, Apollo Global Management and Mulvaney Capital Management - covering managed futures, commodities and macro. He has also worked in operational due diligence at Caliburn Capital Management, a fund of hedge funds. Prior to that, Peter worked in the investment banking industry in a number of senior operational (multi products) and change management roles at ANZ (in New Zealand), Goldman Sachs, Morgan Stanley and JP Morgan.*

*Peter has also advised the Alternative Investment Management Association (AIMA) authoring, or contributing to, the illustrative DDQs for Hedge Fund Managers, CTAs/Managed Futures Managers and Prime Brokers; and the Guide to Sound Practices for Business Continuity Management.*

*Peter holds a Bachelor of Science Degree (Hons) in Physics from the University of Birmingham, is a member of the Chartered Institute for Securities & Investment and is a Chartered Secretary.*

## About KB Associates

KB Associates was established in 2003 and has over 35 professional staff based in Dublin, Cayman and London who support over 100 asset manager clients.

KBA's primary services, out of Dublin, enable asset managers to address the governance, risk, operational and compliance issues associated with the establishment and ongoing management of investment funds. KB Associates services include the following:

- UCITS management function support

- Operational and compliance support including liaison with the Central Bank of Ireland.

- Money Laundering Reporting Officer ("MLRO") services

- Advisory and project management

- Corporate Secretarial services

- Distribution support services

- Irish resident fund directors

- Management Company services under UCITS and AIFMD.

KBA also offers Cayman-based fund directorships and operational consulting services out of London.

The London service includes start-up consulting, helping established managers prepare for operational due diligence, change management, operational reviews and UK Facilities Agent services.

**S1. What KB Associates Does For a Hedge Fund Management Company: Managing the Launch Project**

**S2. Selecting a Provider, including suggested key questions**

# S1. WHAT KB ASSOCIATES DOES FOR A HEDGE FUND MANAGEMENT COMPANY: MANAGING THE LAUNCH PROJECT

## Describe what your firm does for start-up hedge fund managers

KB Associates' work with a start-up client from inception (or soon after) through to fund launch - acting as a "Virtual COO" – responsible for the overarching launch project management. Apart from project management and budgeting, KBA will support the manager with decision-making around fund structure and domicile, the selection and onboarding of service providers, the construction of the business and operational infrastructure (and documentation thereof) and the preparation of investor-friendly marketing and operational documentation.

**MANAGING THE LAUNCH PROJECT**

## 1. OVERARCHING CONSIDERATIONS

### 1.1. What do I Want?

When considering whether to start a hedge fund, the first and most important question is whether you really, really actually want to do it! Not only do you need to have a successful investment strategy but you also need to be prepared to work very hard to establish and then run a business - which presents a host of additional challenges. You will likely need to be the CEO as well as the CIO and are likely to also need to spend a significant amount of time working on business development – i.e. finding investors.

If you find the marketing component too much of a burden and/or irksome at the pre-launch phase you should seriously consider whether you are cut out for the hedge fund business, because both potential and actual investors will demand your time (initially) and the time of your staff. This call on the time of the CIO never goes away – it can be handled in a different way post launch, some of the lower level information flow can be provided by others, but investors will always want some of your time as long as you are managing their money.

Other options such as running a fund as a staffer at an established manager, or going on a platform may be worth considering if you are not convinced that launching an independent asset manager is the way to go.

## 1.2. What do Investors Want

No business can succeed without customers. In this instance the customers are investors. Therefore to be successful you will need to offer them something that they want. Ideally something that they can't easily get elsewhere. This is hard. There are thousands of other hedge funds out there, many undoubtedly with very similar strategies to your own – and then there are numerous other options in the broader asset management industry.

*What are your key distinguishing factors? What is your Unique Selling Point?*

In a tough market for investor capital it is critical to offer an attractive product – and have access to plausible prospective investors. To build it and then hope that they come is a huge risk.

The other thing to consider is the infrastructure requirements of different categories of investor. In general, a High Net Worth Individual will be more tolerant of a basic infrastructure than a large institution. Therefore the infrastructure, including service providers, needs to be constructed with a view as to the likely requirements of the target investor community. More of this later.

Whichever route is taken, a key focus needs to be to make the proposition investor-friendly. This means investing in strong client service, preparing legal documentation that is reasonable from an investor's perspective and having an infrastructure that will pass operational due diligence.

## 1.3. Key Success Factors?

So bringing this together, what are the key success factors required in order to successfully launch a hedge fund? In general, there are four key challenges.

Firstly, the investment strategy needs to be able to deliver risk-adjusted alpha. And this needs to be convincingly demonstrated – either with a track record (or similar) or, where this is not available or cannot be published, other very strong evidence of the fund manager's ability. Examples of the latter would be a significant investment from former employer(s) or a former employer accepting you as a prime brokerage client.

Secondly, the manager needs to have money. This is required to build the business and convince investors, and other stakeholders, that the business has the resources to last at least two years. The manager will also be expected to invest some of their available personal resources in the fund. Now the money does not necessarily need to be the manager's own – a friendly backer will suffice, although these are (i) thin on the ground and (ii) it adds another layer of complexity around ownership, control and the alignment of incentives.

It is difficult to generalise but a suggested initial working capital commitment for a new fund launch in the UK is of the order of £2 million. This should allow the manager to meet the costs set out in 2.1 below, assuming a team of 5 or 6 being paid base salaries, during the pre-launch phase and the first two years of operation. By this stage it should be clear as to whether or not the investment strategy is working and investors are allocating.

Thirdly, as alluded to above, the manager needs to have access to investors. Ideally through their own relationships, but this challenge can be worked around by partnering with skilled and well-networked business developers – either as a partner or in a 3rd party relationship.

Finally, it is important to construct an efficient, robust and credible business and operational infrastructure that will be acceptable to the targeted investors.... and we hope that this book in general and this chapter in particular will set out a realistic path to achieve that.

## 2. BUDGETING

Once the provisional decision to proceed has been taken, the next step should be to prepare a budget. The budget should be split into two sections:

- The Manager
- The Fund(s).

These sections need to then be split into launch costs and ongoing running costs.

### 2.1 The Manager

For the manager, launch costs include:

- Gaining regulatory approval (inclusive of a regulatory consultant).
- Purchase of systems (for example a Portfolio Management System) and market data. Ongoing licence costs may also be significant.
- Staffing (potentially including search fees and legal advice regarding contracts)
- Office Premises (and, if a lease, estate agency, legal advice, office fit out and furniture).
- Office IT and Telecoms Infrastructure set up.

Ongoing costs include, additional to those related to the above:

- Accounting and Payroll
- Tax Advice
- Manager Audit
- Miscellaneous Legal
- Insurances
- Research and Subscriptions
- Travel and Entertainment
- General Office Expenses.

Therefore, although the up-front cost to the manager is likely to be relatively modest, the ongoing annual cost will be far more significant – and the financial resources need to be in place to convince investors and other stakeholders that the business is a long-term going concern.

In order to build an operation with adequate substance for the local regulator, and for investors, it is likely that an annual spend in the multiple hundreds of thousands of Pounds will be required (or other currency equivalent).

Manager costs will normally be expressed in the domestic currency of the manager's jurisdiction and will therefore not necessarily be denominated in Sterling.

### 2.2 The Fund

Fund costs, both launch and ongoing, are normally charged to the investors. Launch costs are typically amortised over a five-year period.

Fund costs will typically be expressed in the base currency of the Fund, so costs incurred in another currency will need to be translated. This is most commonly US Dollars, although the Euro is also popular for EU-domiciled funds.

Initial launch costs include:

- Onshore Legal (e.g. prospectus, investment management agreement and key Service Provider agreements)
- Offshore Legal (including fund establishment and local registration)
- Tax Advice

Ongoing costs to the Fund, additional to the above, may include:

- Fund Administration
- Depositary (if the Fund is an AIF or UCITS)
- Fund Auditor
- Fund Directors
- Manco Directors (if required)
- D&O Insurance
- Brokerage and other transaction costs.

These costs will vary widely dependent on the quality of service providers selected which is, in turn, a function of the prospective investors targeted.

A nascent manager should be aware that the larger the costs that have to be amortised the bigger the drag on returns that investors will experience. To the extent that the investment manager company bears some of the costs the better the net returns will look to investors. Obviously the investment manager company will then have more costs to bear and they cannot be recovered.

## 3. PROJECT MANAGEMENT

Having developed a budget, and hopefully gaining comfort that the costs are realistic and manageable, the next stage is to build a project plan – from inception through to launch.

## 3.1 Key Activities

Below are some of the key activities that will be required to be completed to ensure a successful launch. There is much else but these are the most important.

Many of these activities require the assistance of a relevant service provider

Key activities to go live include:

- Develop the investment strategy, including back-testing and running a shadow book as appropriate.
- Prepare marketing materials.
- Determine fund and manager structure and domicile(s), based on feedback from prospective investors and legal, tax and other advisors.
- Prepare and submit the application for regulatory approval in the manager's jurisdiction.
- Prepare various legal documents underpinning the legal structure, most importantly the prospectus.
- Establish Investment Manager business infrastructure including things like VAT registration, accounting processes and bank accounts.
- Establish operational infrastructure including workflows, controls, governance and procedures.
- Establish risk management infrastructure, processes and documentation.
- Establish IT and telecoms infrastructures.
- Select, buy, test and implement systems – and set up market data.
- Find office space (and kit out if required).
- Hire staff.
- Engage Fund Directors.
- Appoint Prime Broker(s), Counterparties, Executing Brokers, Administrator and Depositary (if required).
- Ensure readiness for investor operational due diligence reviews.

## 3.2 Critical Path and Cross-Dependencies

Critical path items, and ways to mitigate them, are:

- Regulatory application. In the UK, for example, this can take upwards of 6 months from the date of submission. If a rapid launch is required then the workaround – in the UK at least – is to appoint a regulatory umbrella organisation that will allow the manager to invest and market under their licence. This can be set up in a month or two (see chapter 4 from Sturgeon Ventures).

- Office Space. To find an office, agree a commercial lease, fit it out and install the furniture and technology and then move in can take 5-6 months dependent on the size and scope. The workaround is to move into serviced space which can be quickly available. Serviced space is also more flexible in terms of size – but is significantly more expensive, over the lifetime of a lease (typically 5-10 years).

- Hiring of staff. Many personnel are on 3 months (or longer) notice periods. To this must be added the selection process which can easily take several weeks. The workaround is to hire people who are not currently working, or those available on an interim or temporary basis.

- Onboarding of key service providers. The process to select and then onboard service providers such as prime brokers, administrators and portfolio management systems is often fairly complex and time consuming. Allowing for testing can extend the elapsed time to several months. The workaround is to accept, rather than negotiate, unbalanced agreements and to skimp on testing. However both of these options increase longer term operational risk and the future development of relationships with providers

There are several critical-path considerations here. These can include:

- Final regulatory approval is often dependent on having service provider agreements in place. As some of these are dependent on being signed by the Fund Directors then they in turn will need to be appointed and the Fund constituted.

- Regulatory approval will also be dependent on having sufficient substance, which means hiring staff. However, sometimes final hiring decisions are dependent on the level of investor assets expected at launch.

- Investor investment decisions are dependent on operational due diligence – which would include things like reviewing staffing, service providers, regulatory approval and so on.

- Testing of the portfolio management system, the administrator's systems and the prime brokers' systems are mutually dependent – so all need to be ready to go in good time prior to the launch in order that integration testing can be completed.

## 3.3 Managing Risks and Contingency Planning

A well-known saying has it that the "typical" project (not necessarily confined to financial services) takes twice as long and costs twice as much as originally scheduled/budgeted. This is often because many projects are not well-managed utilising professional project management disciplines.

Cross-dependencies have already been discussed but another key discipline is risk management, including contingency planning.

Risk management, in a project management context, means trying to anticipate the "known unknowns" while also allowing for the "unknown unknowns". Every activity will prove more complex than originally anticipated and likely involve additional tasks. Also, many tasks will be undertaken either by or with other people – both internal and external to the business. Misunderstandings, incompetence or lack of availability can cause further delay.

Therefore it is important to, firstly, be very clear about end dates. Are any of these "hard" (e.g. an important launch investor insists that trading starts by a certain date or is there a regulatory constraint)? Secondly, it is important to be realistic about the likelihood of delay – and to build in contingency for this. The danger in trying to hit a deadline if significantly behind schedule is that corners are cut – which in turn increases the risk of subsequent problems.

On the other hand taking away all deadline pressure will likely also result in delays. Therefore it is important both to have a published schedule but, at the same time, be realistic.

Adding in short contingency periods at the end of each phase is good practice. It is also good practice to have risk mitigations in place where practicable. For example, if there is a risk that legal negotiations and testing with an administrator carry a risk of failure, then it would be prudent to at least have commenced discussions with an alternate.

## 4 DOMICILES AND STRUCTURING – THE COMMERCIAL PERSPECTIVE

Legal and tax advisors are highly skilled and can offer very good advice to an investment manager regarding structuring and domiciliation decisions. However, even with the best intentions, this is often weighted towards the managers' interests with insufficient thought given to what the investors want.

Before making a decision as to where to set up the fund(s) it is imperative to consult likely investors as to their needs.

Key questions would include:

- What tax and regulatory constraints are the investors under? Is a double-tax treaty required?
- EU onshore or offshore? Onshore provides the potential benefit of the marketing passport IF EU investors are likely.
- If EU onshore, UCITS or AIF? UCITS has a better established brand but is less flexible and usually slightly more expensive.
- IF EU onshore then one of:
  - Ireland
  - Luxembourg
  - Malta
  - Gibraltar
- Are there likely to be significant US taxable investors (so necessitating a Delaware feeder)?
- If EU offshore, are there preferences between the Caribbean, Bermuda, Channel Islands, Isle of Man – or places like Mauritius and other less known locations?
- Are there any other preferences?

Today, even with AIFMD now in full force and with the extension of the marketing passport to non-EU jurisdictions still likely to be some way off (notwithstanding the progress ESMA is slowly making in this area), the Cayman Islands remains the most popular domicile for funds with a master-feeder model, allowing for immediate or future formation of a Delaware feeder for US taxable investors.

The other matters to consider, from both a manager's and investors' point of view, are:

- Cost
- Time to market
- Perceived robustness of the prevailing regulatory regime (and whether regarded as "equivalent" from the perspective of other regulatory authorities).

# 5 SERVICE PROVIDERS

Before examining the different service provider categories there are a few common themes involving the selection of any service provider that should be considered.

## 5.1 Initial Request For Proposal (RFP)

The first point to emphasise is that competition is generally a good thing! Therefore proposals from several vendors should be solicited, if at all possible. At the very least this keeps the vendors honest, in that they know they will have to come in with a competitive proposal, and it also allows the buyer to compare and contrast different attributes of a proposal.

However, soliciting proposals from too many vendors can, perversely, have a detrimental effect: if the odds of success are long then vendors may not put the same time and effort into their proposal. In general, an optimum number of proposals to request is around 3 to 4.

In terms of how to solicit the proposal, thought should be given as to the detailed requirements in each category. In some areas (e.g. fund administration or prime brokers) AIMA publish DDQs or Guides to Sound Practice which are certainly worth utilising – reputable vendors should have pre-populated completed DDQs. If "blank" proposals are solicited it is likely to become very hard to compare like with like, as well as running the risk of overlooking something important.

## 5.2 Shortlist Selection Considerations

When compiling a short list of 3 or 4 vendors for any particular service provision category, three key areas should be reviewed. There is no "one size fits all solution" – different service providers have very distinct strengths and weaknesses.

Firstly, what is the investment strategy? This is important when considering prime brokers, administrators, portfolio management systems, data vendors and fund directors for example.

Secondly, what is the size and budget of the manager? This should be self-evident but is a common area where mistakes are made. For example, a billion dollar launch will require a very different fund administrator to a $10 million dollar launch – in fact, for this example, the relevant shortlists should be mutually exclusive.

Finally, what is the geography of the investment manager, the fund(s), the invested markets and the core investors? Different providers are strong in different jurisdictions. Does the Administrator have an office, and access to operational detail, in the same time zone as the investment manager.

If inappropriate vendors are approached then the outcome may be to end up with a service provider that is too expensive or cannot/will not provide the service you need and expect. They may also raise concerns with external investors. In some categories there are literally dozens of credible or semi-credible market participants and this is therefore an area were specialist advice really should be sought.

It should also be noted that different categories of investors have different expectations of service providers. An institutional investor will often expect a full slate of "Tier 1" service providers, but smaller investors may be more comfortable with "Tier 2" or "Tier 3" as these will generally be cheaper, may provide a more personal service, and will be a better fit to the budget of the manager/fund. The Total

Expense Ratio (TER) is an important matter too – the fees charged by the top service providers may make the TER for a fund with a low starting AUM uneconomic.

## 5.3 Selection

The selection process commences with preparing a schedule setting out the key criteria previously identified in the RFP document. The response of each tenderer is then noted down and compared. A weighted scoring system could be employed if relevant.

Follow up meetings can then be organised with any vendors who are in with a realistic prospect of success and open issues discussed.

The final selection decision should consider various factors including:

- Cost
- Commercial terms
- Technical capability
- Implementation lead time
- Service levels
- Reputation amongst targeted investors.

It may also be beneficial to take references (including examples of work if relevant), undertake background checks, again if relevant, or undertake full due diligence (investors may do) dependent on the service provider category.

## 5.4 Contracts

It is unrealistic to attempt to drive an exceptionally hard bargain when undertaking final negotiations. An unbalanced contract in the manager's favour, even if agreed, may lead to resentment and poorer service in the longer run – together with a heightened risk of early termination. On the other hand, an unbalanced contract in the service provider's failure is also unsatisfactory. In addition to resentment, potential economic damage and increased operational risk there is also a significant likelihood that prospective investors will balk at the final terms.

Therefore it pays to take time, and potentially legal expense, to negotiate contracts to achieve fair terms. This additional time will need to be allowed for in the overall project plan.

## 5.5 Onboarding

Onboarding may be something as brief as a signed contract and a chat; or a lengthy office design and build, or a full configuration and testing of a portfolio management system.

The onboarding lead times should be discussed and agreed prior to signing the contract. It is particularly important to allow sufficient time for system testing, particularly around portfolio management (and other internal systems), and for going live with the Prime Broker and the Administrator. Insufficient testing increases operational risk.

## 5.6 Service Provider Categories

Detailed below is a fairly exhaustive list of service providers. Not all of these will be required by all managers or funds – but many will be. There is also always the possibility of engaging consultants – either in specialist areas or more broadly to help navigate through the launch process.

### 5.6.1 To the Manager

Accountant

The accountancy provider will likely undertake a variety of roles including book-keeping, VAT reporting, payroll, company secretarial activities and preparation of financial statements.

Auditor

The auditor to the manager, which may be associated with the accountant (above), is responsible for the annual audit of the manager's accounts. This does not need to be same firm which audits the Fund, indeed there are a number of reasons why this may not be appropriate, not least cost. A new Hedge Fund Manager is a small business and the auditor decision should reflect this.

Bank

Every business needs a bank and a hedge fund manager is no exception. Be aware that some banks currently view hedge fund managers as high risk accounts so establishing a relationship may be a little more complex or time consuming than it has been hitherto.

Managers should also consider their treasury needs – and whether or not these can be provided by their bank – or whether another provider is needed for that.

Regulatory Advisor

In order to carry on as an investment manager regulatory approval from the relevant country's host regulator will be required. This is normally a fairly complex and time-consuming activity. In addition, some regulators are running with a long waiting period which makes it is essential that the regulatory application is prioritised – and completed to a high quality. In general, unless significant in-house experience of regulatory applications is available, it makes sense to engage a regulatory consultant. In the UK market, at least, there are many credible options.

## Tax Advisor

While the Fund will probably need tax advice, the manager should also consider their tax position carefully, particularly if the tax status of some or all of the principals is complex. There are several options available in this space – some are strong domestically while others have an international reach.

## Lawyer(s)

In addition to the funds lawyers required for establishing the fund and all the associated documentation, the manager is also likely to require legal expertise in the areas of:

- Corporate
- Commercial
- Property
- Employment

## Recruiters

While some hires may be achievable from the principals' personal contacts others may be harder to realise. Prime Broker consulting teams sometimes offer a "talent intro" service but, in many cases, it will be necessary to engage one or more professional recruiters – either on a contingent basis or on a retained search. There are many recruitment consultancies with expertise in the hedge fund space, as well as many more with broader financial services expertise.

## Real Estate Agent

The investment manager will require office space. Occasionally, this may be available at the offices of another service provider but generally this will have to be sourced independently. In the London market, to use an example, there are two main choices:

1. Serviced space. This has the advantage of being flexible and rapidly available as well as minimising up-front cost. On the other hand, the longer-run cost will be expensive.
2. Acquire a lease. These are typically for 10 years (sometimes with breaks at 3 and/or 5 years) and are cheaper over the long term – but are inflexible and also require an upfront investment in a fit out and furniture. The leaseholder is also usually liable for rates and service charge. Another option is to acquire a shorter term "stub" (i.e. second hand) lease – so for a shorter period - and/or inherit fit out and furniture.

Agents can help with both options. When selecting an agent for lease acquisition take care to ensure that incentives are properly aligned in terms of payment calculations – and also that any possible conflicts of interest, in terms of agents acting for both landlords and tenants, are appropriately managed.

## Office Design and Fit-Out Contractor

If the decision is taken to acquire a new lease then it is likely, although not obligatory, that the tenant will construct their own office fit out rather than inheriting the existing fit out. The industry standard is for space to be returned to Cat A status (i.e. empty) before being re-let. There are many fit out contractors who specialise in offices some of which have a good track record with hedge fund managers.

## Furniture Supplier

Furniture is also likely to need to be independently acquired. It is worth noting that second hand furniture is generally exceptionally inexpensive compared to purchasing new.

## IT Infrastructure

In general, an IT infrastructure will be required and this should be commensurate with the technological demands of the investment strategy. Traditionally this would involve on-site servers although with the advent of cloud computing this has become less important. Cyber-security is now a key consideration, along with an operational, tested business continuity plan.

## Telecommunications

Both land line and mobile telecoms need to be established and specialist vendors can assist with both of these, also incorporating call recording technology and the ability to remotely switch landlines to mobiles in the event of a business continuity incident.

## Portfolio Management and other systems

The Portfolio Management System (PMS) is an integral part of the manager's infrastructure and operational workflow. PMS is a generic term for the various components as below, some or all of which will be purchased from a single vendor although there are plenty of specialists who offer excellent technology for component parts.

- Execution Management System (EMS)
- Order Management System (OMS)
- Portfolio Management System (PMS)
- Risk Management System (RMS)
- Operations Management – trade flow and reconciliations
- Fund and Shareholder Accounting.

Other systems, for example those that support research and analytics, may also be required along with market data terminals.

## Market Data Vendor

Distinct from screens to track markets, market data is required to feed the portfolio management system. This can either be streaming or a series of data points at periodic intervals. Data can be sourced from one or more vendors and a lot will depend on the investment strategy and the number of prices that need to be accessed in order to track the specified investment universe. This cost can become significant.

## Marketing and PR

Help may be required in terms of presenting the firm through its marketing materials, the website and with interacting usefully with the media. Several firms offer these services in all main locations (see Chapter 3 from City Savvy).

### 5.6.2 To the Fund

The selection of many of the below categories of service provider are addressed in AIMA due diligence questionnaires and/or guides to sound practice. These should be reviewed prior to commencing the selection process in order to guide thinking as to what is important in a relationship, and what pointers to look for. If possible, a due diligence questionnaire should be requested along with responses to specific RFP questions that may have been compiled.

Prime or Clearing Broker(s)

To be active in the markets it is important to have a counterparty to trade with – and also someone to custody assets. Prime Brokers will fulfil both these roles – and will also extend credit to finance positions (i.e. leverage), manage margin and will help locate securities to borrow/repo in to cover shorts. Prime Brokers will also receive trades done-away (i.e. with 3rd party brokers) and custody the resultant positions. Other services provided by prime brokers include consulting and capital introductions.

For listed derivatives, a Prime Broker is normally referred to as a Clearing Broker (or Futures Commission Merchant).

It is common for funds to (try to) engage two or more prime brokers in order to ensure that a contingency is in place in case of failure. However, all Prime Brokers will expect to generate a certain amount of revenue from the relationship and small funds may struggle to satisfy more than one prime broker.

## Trading Counterparties and Executing Brokers

Trading counterparties for OTC instruments under an ISDA contract – it is usually difficult to intermediate these back to a prime broker – may be required to ensure best execution is achieved for relevant transactions. These bilateral contracts will need to remain in place with the counterpart for the duration of the transaction.

Executing Brokers for listed and similar products will also be required. These trades will be executed and then given up to the prime broker under a give-up agreement.

## Custodian

In many cases, the Prime Broker will act as a custodian. However, where a PB has not been employed (for example where the fund only acts with direct counterparties and doesn't require leverage or borrowing) then it may be that a separately appointed custodian is required.

## Depositary

Depositaries are required for funds subject to AIFMD or UCITS. If an AIF is non-EU domiciled then it can utilise a "depositary light".

The purpose of a depositary is to safekeep assets, monitor cashflows and oversight, including of NAV calculation. Sometimes depositaries are affiliated to administrators but they can also be independent.

## Administrator

The Fund Administrator is generally regarded as mandatory from an investor's point of view, certainly in Europe and Asia. Its basic role is to independently value the fund's assets and calculate a NAV and to act as the registrar and share transfer agent. Many administrators offer additional services such as regulatory reporting, risk monitoring or outsourced middle and back office.

## Lawyers (onshore and offshore)

The lawyers – both "onshore" (in the domicile of the investment manager or at least in a major financial centre) and "offshore" (in the domicile of the fund) advise on the structure of the fund and then prepare all the relevant documentation (e.g. prospectus, investment management agreement and the memorandum and articles of association of the fund) and ensure that the fund is appropriately incorporated and registered in its home jurisdiction.

## Auditor

The fund auditor will audit the financials of the fund on an annual basis and thereby prove the NAV calculations of the fund administrator. As this is a key backstop role from an investor's point of view it is important that due weight be given to the credibility and brand of the prospective provider – see Chapter 5.

## Fund Directors

The directors of the fund, typically three for a smaller fund, are responsible for representing and protecting the shareholders and ensuring effective governance and decision making at the fund level. At least two of the directors should be independent of the investment manager (and preferably each other). If a master-feeder structure is established then it is common for the directors to sit on both boards.

If an offshore management company is also established then that will need directors also – generally at least two, and preferably not the same people as for the fund.

## 6  BUSINESS INFRASTRUCTURE

A business infrastructure is fairly straightforward to set up and will involve "office management" activities (e.g. HR, procurement) as well as appropriate governance. Traditional business disciplines commensurate with the size and the turnover of the business should be expected. Support can be expected from various service providers, for example the investment manager's accountancy firm.

It is important to ensure that all mandatory legal and regulatory obligations are complied with. Also that robust arrangements are in place for cyber-security and business continuity.

All relevant procedures and controls need to be documented.

## 7  OPERATIONAL INFRASTRUCTURE

The operational infrastructure is a function of:

- The investment strategy
- The portfolio management system
- The fund administrator
- The prime broker(s).

The first step should be to document the process flows, ranging from placing orders, to execution, to confirmation, matching, settlement, corporate events, reconciliation and fund accounting. It will also comprise communication to/from the administrator and prime broker and reporting therefrom.

All relevant procedures and controls also need to be documented.

Attention should also be focused on the month-end process. This includes supporting the Administrator with the NAV calculation, reconciling that calculation and preparing and distributing the month-end bulletins for investors and prospects.

## 8 MARKETING SUPPORT AND PREPARATION FOR INVESTOR OPERATIONAL DUE DILIGENCE

It is absolutely critical that the investment management product is investable from the point of view of the client. In other words, will the manager and fund pass operational due diligence?

The first thing is to ensure that the three key marketing documents present the investment product and manager in the best possible light:

- The pitch book
- The prospectus
- The due diligence questionnaire

These documents should have sound content, be clearly presented, be complete and be consistent with each other. They should give the prospective investor all the information they need in order to undertake initial analysis and ideally move the decision on to the next stage at their end.

Should the investor elect to move to the final stage of the investment process, operational due diligence, then it is important to be well prepared. Investors will expect to see documentation covering all operational, business, risk, valuation and compliance procedures together with all relevant legal documents – and much else besides.

Documents should be credible, reflect the reality of processes at the fund manager, be complete and mutually consistent. It is also important that all documentation, especially legal, should be investor-friendly. Don't give investors an excuse not to invest!

After the documentary review the due diligence process will likely involve a site visit, possibly lasting several hours. Every effort should be made to answer questions accurately, honestly and completely. Investors don't necessarily expect a "perfect" infrastructure from a start-up – but they do expect managers to understand where they need to get to and to see an action plan showing how this will be achieved over time.

**"Probably the most important thing is to ensure that sufficient funds have been attracted prior to launch. It is critically important that the investment manager focuses (near) 100% on portfolio management during the crucial first 6 months."**

## 9 MANAGING THE LAUNCH

Once the necessary approvals have been obtained, the majority of the infrastructure is in place and sufficient assets have been committed it is then time to start the countdown to launch.

A key part of this is ensuring that all the infrastructure has been adequately tested, including with external parties (principally the prime broker(s) and the fund administrator). This should not be rushed and should include activities like carrying out a month end NAV calculation and reconciliation. Depending on the complexity of the strategy this may take several weeks.

The launch plan will likely involve a careful choreography involving the movement of investor funds followed by the commencement of trading. Everyone involved, including at service providers, should know their role in this and how it fits in to the bigger picture.

## 10 CONCLUSIONS

The key conclusion to draw is that launching a hedge fund takes time to do properly. There are many components that need to fit into place before trading can begin – and this needs to be an actively managed project.

However, probably the most important thing is to ensure that sufficient funds have been attracted prior to launch. It is critically important that the investment manager focuses (near) 100% on portfolio management during the crucial first 6 months and is not distracted by prospective investor conversations, marketing trips and the delayed completion of the business and operational infrastructure.

## S2. SELECTING A PROVIDER, INCLUDING SUGGESTED KEY QUESTIONS

KB Associates as a whole is characterised by three things which are important for this work:

- **Independence** – KBA is absolutely independent of the various service providers, receives no referral fees and thus avoids any conflicts of interest.
- **Experience** – Each KBA consultant is professionally qualified and has on average 15 years industry experience.
- **Expertise** – KBA works with many leading investment managers and is active in industry working groups.

The Operational Consulting practice offers expertise, with significant first-hand COO and Operational Due Diligence experience, and provides excellent value for money as:

- The eventual infrastructure will be near-optimal in the context of the client's budget.
- The engagement of KBA enables the client to delay hiring a COO until near launch.
- Knowledge of the various service provider markets enables best value-for-money contracts, appropriate commercial and legal terms and fair service level agreements to be achieved for the client.

41

**Key questions to ask a provider of services in your category?**

- How will you help me successfully launch a hedge fund?

- How much will you charge – and please explain how you can add value?

- How should I approach the challenge if I don't engage you?

- What competitors do you have and what are their relative strengths and weaknesses?

- What costs do you help me avoid?

- Can you give an example of client savings (costs avoided) versus costs of your services?

- Can you impact time-to-market in a hedge fund launch?

**CONTACT INFORMATION**

KB Associates

**Primary Contact:** Peter Northcott, Executive Director

peter.northcott@kbassociates.co.uk

+44 20 3170 8813

**Website:** www.kbassociates.ie

**European office addresses:** 42 Brook Street, London W1K 5DB, UK

5 George's Dock, IFSC, Dublin 1, Ireland

# CHAPTER 3. HEDGE FUNDS AND PUBLIC RELATIONS

By Henrietta Hirst

## About the author

*Henrietta Hirst is a seasoned PR practitioner with more than 25 years experience of advising companies on their international media relations activities, corporate profile raising and issues management. Henrietta has advised companies across a broad range of industry sectors and has experience gained working in the Americas and Australia as well as throughout Europe. Before joining CitySavvy in May, Henrietta ran her own PR company, Parex PR, which specialised in working with clients in hedge funds and the alternative assets industry, and at CitySavvy Henrietta leads the firm's asset management PR practice group in London. Henrietta was previously Managing Director of Group Corporate Communications for United Pan-Europe Communications, Europe's largest cable company. Prior to joining UPC, Henrietta was a Divisional Board Director at Ludgate Communications, the corporate and financial markets communications consultancy, for four years in London and, before that, in New York. She also spent one-year working in-house for the public relations department of the Law Society of New South Wales in Sydney, Australia. Henrietta is an MBA graduate from Cranfield School of Management.*

## About CitySavvy

CitySavvy is an award winning financial PR firm that specialises in providing strategic communications counsel, international media engagement and brand reputation management for asset management sector firms, financial institutions and publicly quoted companies. We have offices in the Netherlands, UK and the US, and the multi-lingual capabilities and campaign experience to help our clients engage with their stakeholders irrespective of time-zone, geography or market cycle.

At CitySavvy we design and execute high-impact, strategic and well-crafted PR and media relations campaigns with an emphasis on accountability and the out-performance of client expectations. In addition to traditional media engagement, we offer specialist expertise in the integration of social and new media platforms, content creation, issues management, and broader multi-disciplinary marketing programmes. Whilst most of our clients retain us on an on-going long term basis, we are also experienced in supporting corporate transactions and fund launches as defined projects.

**S1.Introduction**

**S2. What a PR Company Does For a Hedge Fund Management Company**

**S3. Selecting a PR Company, including suggested key questions**

## S1. INTRODUCTION

Establishing a hedge fund in today's market and raising capital from institutional investors is no easy venture and only the best survive the benchmark three-year threshold. Whilst the flow of new managers launching has remained fairly consistent for the past five years, at roughly 1,000 new managers every year, investors - of all types – are becoming increasingly discerning about and demanding of the managers to which they allocate.

The well-recorded skew in capital flows towards the largest hedge funds is a challenge for new managers. According to leading hedge fund industry data provider, HFR, 69% of global hedge fund industry assets is invested in just 6% of managers – those individually managing $5bn or more – and as the total industry continues to grow, these Billion Dollar firms keep on taking the lion's share of net new capital allocated to global hedge funds.

The institutionalisation of the hedge fund industry has made it more challenging for young managers to grow their businesses. The historical backers of start-up hedge funds (going back to the 1990s and earlier) were Family Offices, private banks and rich private individuals (HNWIs). Institutional investor flows – from pension funds, endowments, foundations and SWFs - became increasingly important throughout the 2000s in the period before the financial markets collapse in 2008, and have been dominant since. Whilst private wealth has come back into hedge funds in the last few years, the total capital in the industry is now dominated by the large institutional allocators and this is unlikely to ever change.

Many of these large investors are averse to investing in start-ups, uncomfortable with the uncertainly and perceived asset insecurity of being invested with a nascent and sometimes unproven manager. Many will be contractually prohibited in their investment mandates from allocating to sub-billion dollar hedge funds or unable to invest in smaller managers because as institutional allocations tend to be larger, their individual 'ticket' would represent too high a percentage of the overall fund assets.

At the same time institutional investors expect institutional standard operational infrastructure and this, coupled with regulatory oversight and compliance, has created a cost burden that many smaller managers struggle to overcome. A recent study by Citi found a typical hedge fund now needs $310 million in AUM to enable its two per-cent management fee to fully pay for its regulatory and operational overheads.

Despite these challenges, capital owners are swamped by pitches from capital-hungry hedge fund managers, both new and established, eager to build their AUM. Distinguishing your firm and fund within the plethora of investment possibilities for the institutional allocator will require your full commitment and marketing savvy. Whilst a solid performance track record is, and always will remain, the single most important element for a successful hedge fund manager to be able to show, this factor is no longer sufficient alone to capture capital commitments. Being able to demonstrate institutional quality infrastructure and processes, a talented and united investment team, rigorous risk management and disciplined investor reporting have also become default requirements. And if a manager cannot successfully communicate these strengths and characteristics, then he (or indeed she) will struggle to survive let alone grow.

Many managers think of the marketing/branding and media elements of the hedge fund business as a luxury, that PR is a non-essential optional 'extra' that few can afford. In short, they think of it as a *Cost* rather than an *Investment*. But the commercially challenging environment articulated above shows that it is this rather old fashioned view of communications that is the luxury that the manager cannot afford!

Within this context, appointing a specialist advisor to help market and promote the launch and growth of a new or early stage fund seems not only logical but eminently sensible. Adopting a well-planned marketing strategy which targets the correct investors in an intelligent manner, can give an emerging or smaller manager the 'edge' that they need to stand out from the crowd, articulate with impact, and gain the attention of capital owners.

So how should the marketing of a new fund be approached and what are the tactics used? Well, working with a sector specialist PR firm is a good place to start.

## S2. What a PR Company Does For a Hedge Fund Management Company

---

**Illustration 1**

**Roles of the Communications Adviser**

Manager and Fund 'identity': determine core messaging and articulation of Fund and manager; visual identity and brand; regulatory compliant marketing, online presence, etc.

Investor marketing: assist with Investment Book and core presentation materials, Fund Fact Sheet, roadshow preparation, presentation training, Q&As

Media relations: identify journalist universe; press outreach; Fund launch release draft and distribution (and follow up activity, as appropriate); ongoing journalist engagement and introductions; forward features and contributed editorial opportunities; media 'point person'

Other activities: conference and event participation by manager; award submissions; issues management and damage limitation (if required); intelligence gathering; sounding board for management team on external perceptions and response

---

### Looking In and Know-Your-Client

*There is so much more that your PR provider, if you've chosen the right one, can do for you than just media relations.* It is a misconception by managers in many industries, not just hedge funds, that PR as a practice is concerned simply with journalist engagement ,but PR - Public Relations - as the words suggest, encompasses outreach to and interaction with all external audiences. Your PR and communications partner should be regarded as a trusted, and often early stage, adviser in much of the same way as a Fund's prime broker, distribution agent or legal counsel will be appointed.

At CitySavvy, the first thing we do if appointed by a new manager is to make sure we fully know and understand our client, their investment proposition and target investors, and help them define their 'edge' within their strategy.  Hedge fund managers are by definition traders and investors, and few have a marketing background or instinct. The chances are they will never previously have needed to articulate their investment approach to the extent they will have to in their new context.

Marketing a new manager or fund should be approached with the same quality of strategic planning and thought as the manager undoubtedly will have applied already to the launch of his or her own business.  A formal communications plan with clear objectives, actions and deliverables should be determined and written down, not least to ensure that proposals can be checked for compliance with relevant regulatory jurisdictions.  This may be particularly vital, for example, for a US manager seeking to launch its first European UCITS fund.

Ensuring the core messaging and pitch points are appropriate – for manager/fund accuracy as well as investor sensitivity – is important. The investment characteristics and appetite of public pension funds and other large institutional investors varies considerably from those of Family Offices or private portfolio wealth managers.  By understanding whom you are selling to, you can write your marketing materials to most effectively resonate with those investors who are the most likely to allocate to your Fund. Use your messaging as a means to differentiate your Fund within an invariably crowded market for competitive products.  Be clear, be concise and focus on addressing those areas of primary concern to your target investors.  It is surprising how many manager waste this opportunity by concentrating on their personal histories, effectively singing their own praises, rather than clearly articulating the investment rationale for their particular fund. Ensure your marketing pitch stands out from the crowd.

The next thing we work on is fund documentation. Core required marketing materials, as a minimum, will be the Investor Presentation and Fund Fact Sheet but can extend to the manager's website and wider online presence (directory listings, LinkedIn page, etc). Presentation of the Fund, whether in written form, visual or verbal pitching, needs to be consistent as well as compliant for regulations across all distribution channels. Working with the right communications partners will allow you to delegate responsibility for developing all of these marketing aspects of your business whilst you focus on fund formation, operational issues, counterparty arrangements and, ultimately, managing the Fund.

**"If there is a single most important marketing activity for the nascent manager to get right it is this – fund launch investor communications"**

At CitySavvy helping new managers with investor pitch materials and non-legal documentation is very much part of our 'day job' and if there is a single most important marketing activity for the nascent manager to get right it is this – fund launch investor communications.

## Looking Out - Engaging the Media

Proactive media relations is a valuable tool available to fund managers hungry to build market profile, brand awareness and assets under management. It is only the most established of managers with closed funds or those running esoteric strategies who perhaps can afford to ignore the media. If you are a smaller or nascent manager - and more than 50% of the global hedge fund industry is populated by firms with less than $100m AUM - investing in media-savvy PR support will help get your name out there and get your Fund written about.

Many managers – but by no means all – will want to do some degree of media activity to announce the launch of their new fund. The press release needs to be written with the same clarity and purpose as the investor materials. New fund launches – unless very large in initial capital or with a 'star' name behind them – do not generally excite journalist interest and many will start life without fanfare, failing to get reported even by the trade media. To counter this it is best to work with a sector experienced PR partner that has a track record of crafting launch announcements that get noticed and create coverage.

Your PR advisor should show that they have a solid knowledge and understanding of the relevant media universe for your story. The financial and investment press is a diverse universe – from dedicated financial media such as the Financial Times and Financial News to the pension fund titles and institutional investor press, to IFA periodicals and those for retail investors, the hedge fund specialist publications, and many others: Do not make the mistake of thinking that blanket distribution is the route to successful coverage but rather segmentation and focus on those titles that will best influence and reach your precise target investors.

Of course, media relations works best if there is a continuum rather than this being thought about as a one-off activity. Post initial launch announcement, try to build a relationship with the journalists who write for and influence the type of investors you are seeking to attract by becoming a helpful source of information and insight for them. Be prepared to speak not just about your individual Fund but about investment trends, investor concerns, industry dynamics and other topics that will help make you an interesting and useful contact. Have an opinion and be prepared to express it. But make sure you consider the audience (readers) for which the journalist is writing and editorial stance of the media outlet concerned as well as the journalist's timeline for filing copy if post interview follow-up is required.

The aspect of a comprehensive media relations programme that most hedge fund managers find the hardest is providing active news flow that sufficiently warrants journalists' attention and to be fair, there is little to say of note about most funds most of the time. If you are to maintain a dynamic dialogue with journalists, your PR adviser will need to be creative about finding and creating valid and valuable opportunities for ongoing media engagement without wasting time, effort or, worst still, dissipating goodwill with idle and ill-thought out approaches. In this respect at CitySavvy, we adopt an assiduous discipline. We consider it fundamental that we know our target journalists and media outlets as well as we know each one of our individual clients and we work hard to ensure there is a beneficial and logical 'fit' between client, media outlet and individual initiative, every time we engage.

The editorial calendars published by the financial, investor and hedge fund media can be very helpful in suggesting key points of journalist outreach during the year and making a note of relevant forward features listed on these is certainly recommended for outreach at the appropriate time. But as a specialist PR consultancy known for our support of asset managers and financial institutions, we are in regular and frequent contact with all the publications of primary importance for our clients and find that most opportunities arise from this direct and individual dialogue.

We also like to suggest that our clients contribute guest editorial and commentary. This is a great way for managers to build recognition of their industry credentials and authority. News media these days are content hungry, especially online, and editors welcome well-written thoughtful editorial from authoritative industry sources.

Getting involved and actively participating in influential networking groups, especially if targeting HNW capital, is another beneficial communications activity. The closely guarded world of Family Office capital can be particularly hard to access. In both the US and Europe, there are a small number of strictly private networks through which Family Office executives (and family members) can come together to exchange views and discuss issues of mutual concern and interest. And on occasion, highly carefully selected asset managers are invited to present at these.

If targeting institutional and pension fund investors there are, of course, much larger, well established and open forums, industry conferences and events to which you can contribute as either a delegate or sponsor or, if you are lucky (and have the right PR partner negotiating for you) be invited to speak as a non-fee paying presenter on the podium or panellist. The right PR partner will be able to help you filter from the wealth of events that are available in order to select the most influential platforms and then work to ensure you 'get a seat at the table'.

Submitting for industry awards can be another useful mechanism to build brand awareness recognising, of course, that winning the award, rather than being shortlisted, will in most instances depend on fund performance and that category success therefore will depend on the skill of your CIO rather than PRO – and so it should!

## Online and social media

The relentless migration of communications to online platforms, news sites and social media creates a challenge for alternative asset managers. For hedge fund managers and others restricted to investment by only qualified and sophisticated investors, we advocate a cautious but well informed stance is adopted, especially with regards to social media platforms – essentially one of 'watch don't play'. This is not the same as suggesting that a manager's own online presence should be ignored. Whatever alternative sources of information may be available to investors, regulators, business counterparties and others, they will always look online. Make sure your website is of the same high quality as your other marketing materials, consistent with

---

**Illustration 2**

**Fund Launch Communications**

**Phase 1: Planning & Preparation**
Communications plan and budget. Determine target audiences. Core description and messaging. Develop investor marketing materials.

Consider and confirm media strategy (exclusive or blanket distribution); write background briefing materials; press release draft, editing and sign-off; compile media targets database; review relevant editorial calendars for post launch media opportunities and set out on PR calendar; decide on media spokespeople and train if necessary; ensure all logos, photos, biogs and/or other helpful materials gathered and accessible; confirm all materials and media plan compliant for regulations

**Phase 2: Day of fund launch**

Press release distribution

D-day interviews

**Phase 3: post launch**

Post launch interviews and press engagement, follow-on activities; forward feature lists and editorial calendars; create written editorial opportunities for client; event speaking platforms; media monitoring

---

the visual look and messaging of these, compliant with all necessary regulatory requirements and restrictions, and kept up to date.

There may be a limit as to how much you wish to put online for either compliance or commercial reasons but the days of the hedge fund manager sheltering behind a single firewall page carrying minimal information - sometimes not even contact details - and purposely promoting a sense of mystique are consigned to the past. The 2012 JOBS Act in the US may not have facilitated a huge uptake in managers marketing and publicly advertising their businesses, but it has led to some making marked improvements to their websites.

## S.3. SELECTING A PR COMPANY, INCLUDING SUGGESTED KEY QUESTIONS

A growing number of hedge funds are appointing external PRs. Rankings compiled by Absolute Return show that 45 percent of the largest North American hedge funds employ a public relations agency, up from 36 percent in 2012. For firms managing in excess of $5 billion, that number leaps to 75 percent.

In appointing PR and communications support – whether an internal hire or outsourced resource – it clearly makes sense to look for a demonstrable track record and knowledge of the hedge fund industry. If appointing externally, working with a smaller consultancy with specific sector expertise and a tighter account team generally provides for a better client experience than choosing a larger agency. Why not speak with your industry contacts about their experiences with different PRs and their knowledge of different agencies, or other fund managers about whether they feel they have obtained value for money through the appointment of a particular PR consultant or consultancy. Seeking the opinion of journalists is another solid approach. Ask them whom they like dealing with and whom they respect on the other side of the fence! Appoint an advisor that you can trust, feel instinctive about and, not least, one that you think you will enjoy working with.

**Key Questions to ask your shortlisted candidate PR firms**

Which other asset management firms/hedge funds do you work for and do you have any client conflicts?

What was the best advice you have given a manager?

How have you helped build a brand name?

What is your fee structure and how much will this cost me?

What success measures do you recommend for our campaign?

What has been your greatest success for a client? What achievement are you most proud of?

Have you ever had any negative client experience and if so, how did this come about and how was the situation resolved?

Is personal fit important to you – have you ever dropped a client?

Who will be directing my account on a day-to-day basis and how senior/experienced are they?

**CONTACT INFORMATION**

**Primary Contact:** Henrietta Hirst

henrietta@citysavvy.com

+44 20 3691 7563

**Website**: www.citysavvy.com

**Address:** 19-21 Hatton Garden, London EC1N 8BA26

# CHAPTER 4. REGULATORY INCUBATION WITH THE PIONEER - STURGEON VENTURES

By Seonaid Mackenzie

## About the author

*Seonaid Mackenzie, the founder and Managing Partner of Sturgeon Ventures, has 32 years' City experience as a stockbroker, fund manager and UK funds operator, as well as fund raising and non-exec appointments for private companies and funds. Seonaid is authorised as an investment manager by the Maltese Financial Services Authority, is on several Maltese self-managed funds' investment committees, and a registered Investment Manager for similar committees in Guernsey. She was on the Strategic Advisory Board of Kleinwort Benson for 2 years.*

*In 2016 Seonaid was awarded "UK – Gamechanger of the Year" at the ACQ5 Global Awards. In 2014 Brummell voted Seonaid one of the top 30 most inspirational female entrepreneurs in UK financial services, while she was a finalist in the American Express 2012 Women of Achievement in the City, and winner of Enterprising Women of 2013, a global award. Seonaid is a Freeman of London with The Worshipful Company of International Bankers, a member of The Chartered Institute of Securities and Investments, the Corporate Finance Faculty of the Institute of Chartered Accountants and the Women's President Organisation (WPO). She has been a guest speaker on financial services careers and being a female entrepreneur at several London secondary schools, topics including her predominantly female workforce of working mothers with flexible hours. She is the founder of the "Wellness Fund Foundation' charity, which focuses on educating parents and teachers on self harm and mental health issues in young persons, and is the angel investor of www.Kidtection.co.uk, a childcare agency for the 21st century with a focus on listening and teens. Seonaid is married and has two school aged children, a puggle and a cocker spaniel.*

## About Sturgeon Ventures

Sturgeon Ventures LLP, founded in 1998, is the pioneer "regulatory incubator" for financial services. Seonaid took the Appointed Representative ("AR") structure used by insurance companies into the wholesale world, creating an innovative structure for investment managers also known as an FCA Umbrella, or Regulatory Hosting Platform. Like all good ideas, others copied it and now there is a host of regulatory incubation firms.

Sturgeon is an SEC Investment Advisor, an AIFM (Alternative Investment Fund Manager) and an Operator of Collective Investment Schemes. To date, Sturgeon has incubated over 100 start-ups.

Sturgeon's team offer regulatory and risk services and a virtual Chief Operating service for fund launches. Its clients include fund managers, third party fund raisers, corporate finance firms and family offices. Sturgeon works with law, compliance and accountancy firms, prime brokers, custodians and pension consultants, assisting firms to set up funds in Malta, Dublin, Cayman, Luxembourg, Gibraltar and the UK. As a MiFID firm, it can give corporate finance advice, can manage managed accounts, and be delegated to as a manager by full AIFMs across the EU, both by UCITs managers, on-and-offshore, and by offshore self-managed funds.

Sturgeon is also a sub-threshold AIFM, directly managing unleveraged closed-ended funds, and delegated to by AIFMs and UCITs Management Companies and smaller sub-threshold hedge funds. Post-Brexit, Sturgeon's flexible structure will enable it to continue its full range of services with EU domiciles.

Sturgeon Ventures LLP recently won ACQ5 2015 Regulatory Hosting Platform, Family Office Wealth Advisor and International Business Strategy Consultancy of the year.

**S1.What a Regulatory Hosting Firm Does For a Hedge Fund Management Company**

**S2. Selecting a Regulatory Hosting Firm, including suggested key questions**

# S1.WHAT A REGULATORY HOSTING FIRM DOES FOR A HEDGE FUND MANAGEMENT COMPANY

## 1. BRANDING

As a start-up, you can either create a name yourself, or you can choose a branding consultant to help you to select a name and develop a brand. If you require contact details for a branding consultant, we do know some, but I usually say "find a story that tells your story." I have even had companies join their children's names together. It illustrates our commitment that for one client I researched and designed their logo for them in my spare time. Your brand is important as it will usually be your first slide. Many say to me "Why Sturgeon?", and it is a great opening line; we have a story.

How do I check whether my chosen name is available? Before launching a new hedge funds business, it is extremely important to ensure that the names or trademarks you propose to use for your management business and funds do not overlap with existing names which are in use or with registered trademarks.

It is worthwhile spending time to determine whether earlier trademarks exist that are similar to your chosen name. It can be a very costly and disruptive exercise to undergo a change in branding if you discover such a similarity after launch.

In order to ensure that your brand identity is not vulnerable to claims of trademark infringement or passing off, you should at a minimum:

- search for your proposed name using an internet search engine. This should provide an immediate indication as to whether your chosen name is already in use and what sort of business is using it (note that even where a business using the name is operating in a different space, this could still be a problem)

- carry out a search of Companies House using the WebCheck service. You should also refer to the Companies House publication Incorporation and Names which gives useful guidance on acceptable names, and

- instruct a trademark search to be carried out to check for registered trademarks applicable to the UK and any other territories where the name will or may in the future be used - although trademark registries are accessible online, the scope of trademark rights is a highly technical issue so it is not safe to proceed without taking expert advice on this issue - we work with teams of trademark and brand protection specialists who will be pleased to advise.

If you wish to name your funds and your investment management business entities consistently, you should also consider carrying out a check of any relevant registers in the country in which your fund entities will be domiciled, to ensure that your chosen fund names are available for use.

It is equally important to determine which other businesses are using or have trademarks registered for your proposed name or similar names. What counts as "similar" in connection with trademarks and passing-off can be wider than expected, and, as indicated above, the rights which third parties may have to prevent use of names similar to theirs may also extend much further than is readily apparent - in some circumstances owners of rights in entirely different sectors can prevent use of a name for a fund or a related entity.

Do I need to protect against others using the name and brand I have chosen? Yes. It is also better to have ®in your logo; it means you have thought about it. You should also ensure that your name and reputation are not appropriated by others to your detriment in the jurisdictions in which you wish to operate, for example you could check the register of Cayman Islands mutual funds.

It is therefore highly advisable to protect your business's trading name(s) (including fund names) against third party use, through trademark registrations in appropriate jurisdictions. A trademark can consist of the distinctive element of the name of a fund or business, a trading name, a logo, or a combination of any of these. It could, for example, be applied to the business's website and/or any related materials acting as a means of identifying the website as that of the fund manager, and distinguishing it from any other similar sites. As with trademark searches, you should obtain professional assistance to apply for trademark registrations, or it is pretty easy to do it online yourself, Sturgeon have done a blend: we use professional consultants and have also done it online.

## 2. REGULATORY POSITION

Under a regulatory umbrella arrangement you (as CIO of your firm "ABC") would be an appointed representative (AR): an AR is exempt from being regulated by the Financial Conduct Authority ("FCA"), and is instead effectively indirectly regulated by the regulatory host (or principal). To become an AR as an investment manager firm, ABC enters into an appointed representative agreement with a regulatory host, in this case Sturgeon. That agreement covers the activities that ABC as an AR is permitted to perform directly with its own clients. Those activities include investment advice and fund marketing (described by the FCA as "arranging"), but do not include discretionary investment management or managing a hedge fund. Therefore, to work within the regulatory framework, the new AR (i.e. ABC) seconds its individual investment manager(s) to Sturgeon as the regulatory host, and that arrangement is covered by a secondment or consultancy agreement between the regulatory host and the individual investment manager. Those individuals are registered by Sturgeon with the FCA as its approved persons. This is why your client agreements will have both Sturgeon and ABC as parties, as investment manager and adviser respectively, with the individuals making the investment decisions for the client as regulated consultants of Sturgeon.

As an AR, ABC will therefore be able provide advisory services with its own brand and the same individuals can provide discretionary investment management services for ABC's clients or manage a fund for underlying investors whilst within Sturgeon Ventures. The firm ABC is not directly regulated by the FCA, rather your firm is hosted via Sturgeon for advisory and marketing services. Sturgeon itself is directly authorised and regulated by the FCA and has a range of regulatory permissions which include investment management and investment advice. Sturgeon acts de facto as your regulator for the advisory and marketing work and monitors your activities from a risk and compliance perspective.

There is no specific code for "a regulatory umbrella" as such, and the legislation relating to ARs is quite technical, but it amounts, in summary, to the above.

## 3. FUND STRUCTURE

Sturgeon has a lot of experience in fund structuring. However, Sturgeon is not a legal advisory firm. Instead, Sturgeon explains fund structure options to clients from a position of experience, and then works closely with legal counsel in all fund jurisdictions around the globe to procure deal-specific legal advice.

Finding out the fund structure and domicile that suits your strategy and investor base is important at the start, and will impact the ability of the fund assets to grow. Together with legal and tax counsel, Sturgeon will assist you in developing a proposition that can be used to set up the fund structure, a set of managed accounts, and help to frame your overall structural choices. The options will include, in particular, whether to be an onshore AIF or offshore AIFM, and whether to be self-managed or not. There are decisions to be made on the domicile of the fund entities, which may well reflect where you wish to market your fund(s). For the EU this is assisted by our educational website www.aifmsolutions.com.

The majority of hedge funds of our clients are domiciled in the Cayman Islands. The launch process for a Cayman Islands or other "offshore" domiciled fund is relatively quick and straightforward and ongoing obligations are generally less onerous than for funds domiciled in European jurisdictions. However, certain investors, including large and European institutional investors, may request that a fund entity be domiciled in Europe due to a number of factors, including such investors' familiarity with the relevant jurisdiction, restrictions on the jurisdictions in which they may invest and/or a perception that a European fund is better regulated. Further, the implementation of AIFMD means that where a European hedge fund manager manages European domiciled funds (for example, Luxembourg, Malta and Ireland), such funds can now take advantage of an EEA-wide passport for marketing to professional investors. By contrast, Cayman Islands domiciled funds (and other non-EEA domiciled funds) can currently only be marketed to professional investors within the EEA if the fund has been registered with the relevant member state, and/or potentially has a depositary and is then acting within the confines of the private placement rules of the relevant member state.

## 4. USING THE FUND STRUCTURE TO BUILD A TRACK RECORD

Attracting investors can best be done in the context of creating an actual fund structure. Having an audited opinion based on statements from different independent service providers, gives potential- investors a high degree of comfort.

Establishing a fund also allows for operational efficiency when dealing with a larger group of investors or investors from different jurisdictions, while also enabling a demonstration to investors of experienced operational oversight. Depending on the location of the investment team, the investor base and future growth plans, Sturgeon then engages in conversations with all relevant entities about the most appropriate fund structure, where issues relating to regulation, transparency and fiscal treatment will all play a determining role. Sturgeon's team are very focused on governance and monitoring and oversight not just of you as the manager but all the service providers of the fund and investors find this aspect very positive. Sturgeon have already taken part in countless due diligence sessions with pension consultants and other fund due diligence teams, and thus far passed, so making this is an invaluable tool for a start-up manager.

## 5. DOCUMENT COMPLIANCE

Sturgeon's team is highly experienced in assisting managers in preparing their marketing documentation, both providing detailed practical advice on content and approach, and also ensuring it is in line with FCA and EU rules, with appropriate disclaimers added on.

## 6. ADVICE ON MARKETING SCOPE

"Where can I market?" is a common question. Sturgeon has a close handle on marketing developments throughout the EU and other global jurisdictions and can share these updates with you. It depends on the jurisdiction of the fund, its size and each country's rules.

## BENEFITS OF USING A REGULATORY UMBRELLA

The benefits here are many, but the principal ones are timing and cashflow, as well as advice on running a new business and the potential for capital introduction. It takes on average around one to two weeks for an individual to become an authorised person (a CF30) within Sturgeon and its AR. The firm is normally up and running as the Appointed Representative (AR) within a matter of days. By contrast, to get directly authorised by the FCA can take on average 6-9 months, depending on the strategy and business, with complex ownership structuring typically adding several weeks' additional review time per layer of ownership). We have seen one authorisation take 18 months where unusual control and history circumstances were involved. During this review time you can neither raise funds nor manage them if they arrive before authorisation, so the AR structure is extremely important.

Under a regulatory umbrella there is no regulatory capital to put up, although you do need to submit management accounts of your AR to Sturgeon. By contrast, the Regulatory Capital requirement for a UK advisory firm with no EU Passport is £5,000. A CAD Exempt firm which has the passport as a corporate advisory firm is €50,000 and a MiFID investment management firm with a passport is €50,000 or 25% of operating costs - whichever is the higher. If a firm goes on to be a full AIFM it is a minimum of €125,000. Of course the other added saving is on an in-house compliance officer and anti-money laundering officer, whose salaries today are even for a small firm upwards of £60,000, with rising

> "The principal benefits of using a regulatory umbrella are timing and cashflow, as well as advice on running a new business and the potential for capital introduction."

Professional Indemnity insurance, as their job becomes increases risky with ever more regulatory changes.

Being under the umbrella of Sturgeon, you will learn how to run a regulated business from day one, whilst having a very experienced team alongside you to educate, nurture, and govern. There is also the possibility of introducing assets from other Appointed Representatives within the Sturgeon family and Seonaid's 30 years of experience and contacts has frequently proved invaluable in assisting with fundraising. Within that family are a number of Appointed Representatives that are family offices, and Sturgeon also manages family money. Sturgeon has also seen individual ARs investing in another AR's fund as a result of Sturgeon's focus on relationships and introductions.

## US MARKETING ADVANTAGES

Sturgeon Ventures is also fully SEC regulated, which means that all portfolio managers within Sturgeon can market in the US to qualified investors.

There is also a marketing specific bonus in working with Sturgeon. More than 50% of Sturgeon's team are working mothers, and the firm is owner managed with the majority of the firm owned by a woman. Therefore you have a Portfolio Manager of your fund with a strong diversity tick. This matters especially if you are speaking with US pension funds.

## PRICING

For most clients/funds, Sturgeon's pricing is calculated based on the number of Appointed Representatives in the firm. However, on the closed-ended funds there is an element of funds-under-management, and the pricing is then calculated on a number of different elements, such as basing the fee on the number of funds launched where there are no individual ARs.  The delegated model described above is still the best option for a start-up manager, with a sub-threshold AIFM is still cheaper than a full AIFM.

Sturgeon's clients have a minimum 6 month contract, which then extends further with rolling notice periods, but offering the option for immediate termination upon the client firm becoming directly authorised, or else enabling the client to continue working with Sturgeon's compliance services post-authorisation.

Now that competition has given start-ups a choice of incubatory provider, potential clients may argue for a cheaper solution. However, it should be noted that all the competitor firms use Sturgeon as a benchmark, so implicitly acknowledging its status, while claiming to be cheaper and more flexible, although their service range and experience tends to be far inferior.

When looking at pricing, one element muddies the water: Sturgeon insists on Professional Indemnity insurance for all their ARs, once AR status has been achieved. Not all of Sturgeon's competitors insist on PI, and therefore their fees are likely to appear cheaper.  However, this means that both client and umbrella firm are then exposed to potentially material liabilities.   It should be remembered that Sturgeon, in requesting this, is the most experienced firm in this sector.


## S2. SELECTING A REGULATORY HOSTING FIRM, INCLUDING SUGGESTED KEY QUESTIONS


Experience in this area is our most important intangible asset as a business. At the time of writing Sturgeon has incubated in excess of 100 start-up firms.

Sturgeon is one of the few regulatory incubators with its own in-house experienced fund managers all regulated today as CF30s, perfect for a one man band, needing experienced people around them, or for disaster recovery should something happen to a manager.

Sturgeon works with many compliance consultancies, both the ones that have crept into Sturgeon's space and started copycat regulatory umbrella offerings, and those who have stayed true to just consultancy, so you are not constricted in selecting your other service providers. Before making any appointment, the new firm should check a firm's permissions: this is easy on the FCA's Register. The key checks are to see whether the firm is a MiFID firm, a sub-threshold or a full AIFM. Do they have the EU Passport as a MiFID firm for marketing, or can your fund be passported across the EU because you have appointed a full AIFM or UCITS manager who has delegated back to a firm like Sturgeon, enabling your AR to then undertake the marketing activities.

It is also fundamental to find people you like, because at the end of the day, they are part of your documents, and they are a partner team during the incubation. Experience is key: have the principals of the hosting firm ever managed funds themselves, or more importantly successfully raised capital?

Postpartum - What happens after your start-up firm obtains independent authorisation with the FCA? In the case of Sturgeon, the

> **"Experience in regulatory hosting is our most important intangible asset as a business. At the time of writing Sturgeon has incubated in excess of 100 start-up firms."**

team is always happy to continue as part of your ongoing compliance team, or hand you back to the compliance firm that originally introduced you to Sturgeon, or else help you find a compliance officer and simply be there for ad hoc high level advice. Seonaid Mackenzie has been known to stay on investment committees after breakaway due to the strength of her little pink book and her passion for governance - and of course the diversity tick.

## ADDED STRENGTHS OF THE STURGEON OFFERING

The Sturgeon added value includes resources across media that are made available to clients. Each client has a dedicated account person as a primary source, but this is backed up with an extensive library of material to help you understand the processes of setting up and help with your decision making.

Lastly Sturgeon has a passion for education, and recently launched an education website. www.aifmsolutions.com which has many useful articles for the start-up hedge fund manager. Do also check out Thomson Reuters Podcasts with Seonaid as a speaker in "How to start a hedge fund".

We at Sturgeon walk-the-walk not talk-the-talk, we are entrepreneurs helping other entrepreneurs. We are owner-managed, with no outside investor and no debt, with never a loss-making year. The key to being that entrepreneur is to have persistence, passion and belief. The skill to grow a great team. I once heard another entrepreneur say: "Don't follow the herd, look for a ground floor opportunity that will give you most potential to shape the market and when you have reached the top, send the lift down for the others". Sturgeon pioneered a paradigm shift for start-ups to use hedge fund incubators in 2000, the rest is history.

Sturgeon's mission statement: to provide world class advice and solutions that create lasting relationships.

KEY QUESTIONS TO ASK YOUR POTENTIAL REGULATORY UMBRELLA PROVIDER

How many firms have you hosted?

How long does an incubatee firm stay with your firm?

What factors cause them to leave?

How many former clients using the regulatory umbrella service used that firm for other services after independence?

Can I speak to current and former clients?

What experience and qualifications do your team members have in the industry?

## CONTACT INFORMATION

**Primary Contact:** Seonaid Mackenzie

sm@sturgeonventures.com

**Alternative Contacts:** Alexandra Brown

ab@sturgeonventures.com

or Tom Powell

tp@sturgeonventures.com

Switchboard number: +44 20 3167 4625

**Websites:** www.sturgeonventures.com, www.aifmsolutions.com

**Address:** Linstead House, 9 Disraeli Road, London SW15 2DR

# Chapter 5. Setting Up A Hedge Fund In Europe – The Auditor and Accountant's Perspective

By Bernadette King and Melanie Pittas of haysmacintyre

## About the authors

*Bernadette King has advised businesses in the financial services sector for over fifteen years and is Head of Financial Services for award-winning chartered accountants haysmacintyre, which includes over 100 fund managers in its client portfolio. Bernadette is a member of the ICAEW's FS Faculty and 100 Women in Hedge Funds.*

*Melanie Pittas is a partner within haysmacintyre's financial services sector team with over ten years' experience of working with FCA regulated entities. Melanie is a regular attendee of AIMA events.*

*[It is important to note that content has been authored following the result of the UK referendum on leaving the EU (23 June 2016). Any compliance requirements and rates quoted may be subject to change.]*

## About haysmacintyre

haysmacintyre is a leading mid-tier firm of Chartered Accountants and Tax Advisers with a team of 30 partners and over 230 people working together in one central London office, providing advice to entrepreneurs, fast-growing businesses, listed and regulated entities, charities and not for profit businesses across the UK and internationally.

We are among only a few firms who are able to bridge the gap between the largest firms which "do Everything", but lack the personal touch, and smaller firms that are only able to provide a narrow range of services.

In 2014, we were named Mid-Tier Firm of the Year at The British Accountancy Awards which recognises our client service, the quality of our delivery, our people, innovation and commitment to the sectors we service. In 2015, we were a finalist in the 'Employer of the Year' category of The British Accountancy Awards and in the 2016 competition, shortlisted for the 'top 50 audit team of the year' award.

**S1. What an Accountancy Firm/Auditor Does For a Hedge Fund Management Company**

**S2. Selecting an Accountancy Firm/Auditor, including suggested key questions**

# S1. WHAT AN ACCOUNTANCY FIRM/AUDITOR DOES FOR A HEDGE FUND MANAGEMENT COMPANY

## INTRODUCTION

As with many new businesses, the likelihood of future commercial success can be influenced by decisions made early on, but while in many sectors business owners can enjoy a substantial degree of free-will, those operating in the financial services arena are bound by regulation.

The advice of a sector specialist auditor can ensure from the onset that a hedge fund manager start-up makes the very best use of the options available to it and complies where its choices are limited.

This chapter provides an overview of the start-up considerations and immediate financial and other reporting requirements a fund manager has when setting up a business in the UK and offers recommendations on how best to deal with these requirements.

## COMPANY SET-UP: COMPLIANCE ISSUES, WHAT STRUCTURE IS BEST

**When you set up a business the structure you adopt influences your ongoing compliance requirements. Here we set out some of the options available to a fund manager start-up and the responsibilities that are associated with them,**

### COMPANIES HOUSE AND YOUR LEGAL RESPONSIBILITIES

It is relatively straightforward to set up a new limited company or limited liability partnership (LLP) in the UK, but the ongoing compliance obligations can be considered increasingly onerous.

Registration with Companies House can be achieved by using the on-line facility on the gov.uk website or by engaging a professional adviser to do so on your behalf. A new company must have Articles of Association setting out the rules by which it will be governed and usually the standard Model Articles of Association, which can be found online, will suffice. For some companies, however, it may be more appropriate to have bespoke Articles and an adviser should be consulted on this matter. LLPs will not have any Articles of Association, but it is recommended practice to enter into an LLP Agreement; a private document which does not need to be filed with Companies House.

Useful information on how to set up and run a company or LLP is available on the gov.uk website.

**Ongoing compliance obligations**

The trade-off with having limited liability is the requirement to publicly disclose information about the entity. Filing documents late is an offence under the Companies Act and directors/LLP members can be prosecuted and fined. A history of late filing can also have an adverse effect on a company's credit rating.

Below is a summary of the ongoing filing obligations of a limited company/LLP with Companies House.

---

**Ongoing filing obligations with Companies House**

- Financial accounts must be filed within nine months of the year end to avoid any late filing penalties
- A confirmation statement (previously known as the 'annual return') must be submitted at least once every 12 months
- Appointments and resignations of directors/LLP members and their personal details, as and when they occur

- A change of registered office address
- A change of accounting year end
- Any new share allotment or changes to the share capital structure (limited company only)
- Certain members' resolutions as well as any revised Articles of Association (limited company only)
- Auditor resignation or removal

---

## Directors' duties

Directors' duties and responsibilities is a complex subject, the details of which are beyond the scope of this chapter and a matter on which advice should be taken. Provided here as a starting point are the statutory duties outlined in the Companies Act with which directors should be familiar. Designated members of LLPs should also comply with these duties as far as they are applicable.

---

**Directors' statutory duties**
- Act within powers in accordance with the company's constitution
- Promote the success of the company for the benefit of the members as a whole
- Exercise independent judgment
- Exercise reasonable care, skill and diligence
- Avoid conflicts of interests
- Not to accept benefits from third parties
- Declare any interests in proposed transactions or arrangements

---

Directors can incur personal liabilities if they breach their duties. This can result in being disqualified from acting as a director. A director found guilty of wrongful or fraudulent trading can be made personally liable for a company's debts.

## Corporate governance and statutory records

It is recommended practice to establish a robust corporate governance framework from the start. Even for small companies, the framework should incorporate the various legal obligations and establish a regular meeting and reporting cycle. Although not a legal requirement, it is often useful to appoint a company secretary who can take charge of tasks such as maintaining the statutory books and registers and advise the directors of their duties.

## Company stationery and premises

Business letters, emails and websites must as a minimum show a company's or LLP's full name, the part of the United Kingdom in which the entity is registered, for example, England or Wales, the company number and the registered office address. The company name must also be displayed at the registered office, the place of trading (if different) and any place where company records are available for inspection.

## People with Significant Control register

UK companies and LLPs are required to maintain a register of People with Significant Control (PSC Register) and to make the information public by filing it with Companies House. Companies must take reasonable steps to identify PSCs and must keep the register up to date as and when changes occur. The information must be filed with Companies House at least once per annum. Failure to comply with these rules is a criminal offence which can result in fines or imprisonment. Details of those considered Persons with Significant Control are given below.

---

**A Person with Significant Control is an individual who directly or indirectly meets one or more of the following conditions in relation to a company or LLP**

- Directly or indirectly owns more than 25% of the shares (for LLPs, holds rights over more than 25% of the surplus assets on a winding up)
- Directly or indirectly holds more than 25% of the voting rights
- Directly or indirectly holds the right to appoint or remove the majority of directors (for LLPs, holds the right to appoint or remove the majority of those involved in management of the LLP)
- Otherwise has the right to exercise, or actually exercises, significant influence or control

---

> - Has the right to exercise, or actually exercises, significant influence or control over the activities of a trust or firm which is not a legal entity, but would itself satisfy any of the first four conditions above if it were an individual

The register should include the name of the PSC and their service address, home address, date of birth, nationality, the date when he or she became a Person with Significant Control and which conditions for being a Person with Significant Control are met. The register must never be empty and fixed statutory wording is available to cover various circumstances, for example where there are no PSCs or where the company has not yet managed to obtain the full information required for its PSCs.

If a company is controlled by a legal entity which is subject to the PSC rules or similar disclosure requirements then the details of the parent company should be inserted in the register. If not, then it will be necessary to look at the ownership and control of that legal entity to identify any individuals or entities who have a majority stake in that legal entity and who might therefore need to be registered as a PSC. Entities exempt from the PSC requirements are given below.

> **Entities exempt from the PSC requirements include**
> - Companies that are subject to Chapter 5 of the Financial Conduct Authority's Disclosure and Transparency Rules
> - Companies listed on a regulated market in the UK or European Economic Area (other than the UK) or on specified markets in Switzerland, US, Japan or Israel
> - Limited Partnerships

The Department for Business, Innovation & Skills (BIS) has produced guidance on the PSC requirements for companies and LLPs as well as separate statutory guidance on the meaning of "significant influence or control". These guides are available on the gov.uk website. It is recommended that advice it sought from a professional adviser with company secretarial or legal expertise to assist with interpretation of the detailed rules, which can be complex depending on the specific circumstances.

## WHAT BUSINESS STRUCTURE IS BEST?

If the first requirement of any business structure is limited liability (without this protection against failure many businesses would not assume the commercial risks necessary to succeed) the choice of available structures is reduced to either a Limited Company or Limited Liability Partnership (LLP). Both are corporate bodies having separate legal personality and both provide limited liability to their shareholders or members.

This does not mean that the choice of structure is therefore determined by whether a corporate or partnership business ethos is favoured. Many LLPs are managed by a board of their senior members on corporate lines while equally many Limited Companies are managed on a more inclusive basis, as quasi-partnerships; the choice of structure may facilitate a preferred management style, but it does not determine it.

Flexibility is perhaps the foremost requirement of any business structure: the ability to accommodate the changing commercial requirements of the business and its owners over time and on a tax efficient basis. In this the LLP enjoys an advantage over the Limited Company in as much as it has no share capital (and therefore shareholders) and is not subject to capital maintenance requirements; both characteristics which contribute to the LLP's comparative flexibility in a number of important respects.

## Flexible profit allocation

The profits of an LLP may be allocated on a wholly discretionary basis in accordance with arrangements provided for in its Members Agreement (which is not a public document). Profits may therefore be allocated on a different basis annually or on different bases dependent upon the nature of the profits themselves: whether capital or revenue or to distinguish between profits derived from different profit centres. The allocation of profit by a Limited Company is necessarily constrained by the fixed shareholding percentages held by the shareholders (although this can be overcome to some degree by arranging for different classes of share, so called alphabet share arrangements, to be held by different groups of shareholders).

## Return of funds generally to members

Subject to the cash being available and FCA approval, if appropriate, the LLP may freely distribute profits, advance loans and return capital to members with minimum formality. The Limited Company, subject as it is to capital maintenance rules, requires available reserves to distribute profits and must meet restrictive company law requirements in making loans and returning share capital to shareholders whether by way of share buyback or liquidation. Such loans or return of funds to shareholders will generally involve a tax cost.

## New members

A further flexibility available to the LLP is the ease with which new members may be admitted (and conversely, members removed); the simple execution of a deed of adherence to the Members Agreement is sufficient to introduce a new member. This compares with the relative difficulty in introducing new members in a Limited Company (in terms of funding the acquisition of shares for the new shareholder or in the dilution of other shareholders' interests) and of removing director shareholders and in recovering their shares (involving employment rights issues, the valuation and funding of the purchase of the departing shareholder's shares and the destination of such purchases).

## Tax neutrality

The above flexibilities are available to the LLP on a tax neutral basis. The distribution of profits, the return of capital, the introduction and removal of members may all be achieved without tax costs for the LLP or its members. This tax neutrality results from the fact that the LLP is a tax transparent entity, as discussed next. By comparison, the payment of dividends, the return of capital, the transfer of shares between members, the admission of new shareholders on favourable terms are all occasions of potential tax charge to shareholders.

## Tax transparency of a Limited Liability Partnership

An LLP is a corporate body, albeit described as a partnership because of its particular company law attributes. Most significantly it is treated as a partnership for tax purposes and therefore, as with partnerships generally, it is tax transparent. As a tax transparent entity the profits of the LLP are charged directly on its members (partners) as they arise (are recognised in the accounts) and irrespective of whether those profits are distributed or retained in the business. As the profits of the LLP are taxed on the members on an arising basis and at their marginal rate of income tax (which may be 47% for an additional rate tax payer) their subsequent distribution by the LLP has no tax significance. Hence the tax neutrality of the LLP. If all the profits have been taxed as they arise then what happens thereafter is of no tax significance.

## Better rates and reliefs

In contrast, a Limited Company is taxed independently from its shareholders and pays corporation tax at a rate of, currently, 20% on its taxable profits. These rates are anticipated to fall to 19% with effect from April 2017 and 17% from April 2020. There is no tax charge on the shareholders until those profits are distributed as dividends or returned on a liquidation when further tax costs at the shareholder level will result.

The limited company therefore offers a material tax deferral (of as much as 27%) as compared to the members of an LLP where the individual might be paying income tax at a marginal rate as high as 47%. In addition to the potential tax deferral benefits afforded by the Limited Company, it is also the case that, increasingly, tax reliefs are targeted toward Limited companies, for example, the LLP does not qualify for reliefs such as R&D tax credits.


## Conclusions to be drawn

The flexibility and tax neutrality of the LLP must be weighed against the potential tax deferral benefits of the Limited Company, which will be particularly relevant where profits are to be retained in the business in order to fund working capital or other business investment. It should also be recognised that an LLP cannot be listed and the sale of an LLP may not maximise the value of the business while many purchasers still regard an LLP (perhaps unfairly) with some suspicion when it comes to making a corporate acquisition.

Recent changes to restrict tax planning opportunities for "mixed partnerships" (typically a LLP with a corporate member or members) have seen a shift in favour of the company by hedge fund managers from the former pre-eminence of the LLP. However the shift has not been sufficiently marked to conclude that the poles have reversed, just that the decision has become more finely balanced. By default it may be preferable to favour the LLP on the basis that it is relatively simpler to incorporate an LLP into a Limited Company than to dis-incorporate should the structure need to be changed. Ultimately, any decision will rest upon individual circumstances and may even, as suggested earlier, extend to such 'soft' issues as to whether a partnership or corporate ethos more accurately reflects how the owners wish to conduct their business.

## THE FIRST TWELVE MONTHS: YOUR ACCOUNTS, AUDIT AND VAT RESPONSIBILITIES

**Following set-up, it is natural that the fund and its performance will be a priority for you. The success of the fund will be undone, however, if the fund manager business fails to deliver on its regulatory and legal responsibilities. Here we provide an overview of your reporting responsibilities.**

### PRODUCTION OF YOUR COMPANY ACCOUNTS

If your finance function is outsourced much of the following will be taken care of by the provider, but as noted above business owners have ultimate responsibility for the preparation of the accounts and adherence to applicable reporting requirements lies with the directors and LLP members and this section provides an essential overview of the decisions and actions required.

Businesses must select an accounting reference date (ARD) and update Companies House, if necessary as on incorporation Companies House will default a business's ARD to be the month in which it incorporated. An ARD can be any date of the year and most common year ends in the financial services sector are: 31 March, 30 June, 30 November and 31 December. Before selecting the ARD, tax advisers should be consulted as in some cases (particularly for LLPs) there are tax implications to the date chosen as, for example, the date could affect overlap relief for an LLP. The decision needs to be taken in conjunction with the first anticipated receipt of a performance fee and then delivery must follow a timetable, which if not applied can result in prosecution and fines.

---

**Accounting timetable and first filing of accounts**
- An accounting period can be any length of time up to 18 months, but there are restrictions on repeatedly lengthening the ARD
- An entity has 21 months from the date of incorporation to file its first accounts at Companies House, even if the ARD has been extended to 18 months
- For accounting periods thereafter, the entity has nine months from the ARD to file the accounts at Companies House
- Currently, paper copies of the accounts are filed at Companies House

---

*THE INITIAL AUDIT AND SPECIAL REQUIREMENTS*

A statutory audit is required if the entity is FCA regulated. The FCA can give clearance, however, on a business about to be wound-up not requiring an audit.

## Financial Conduct Authority and Gabriel portal

An auditor will undertake a separate assignment as part of the audit process in order to make a limited assurance report on client assets to the Financial Conduct Authority (FCA). Audited accounts, together with this report, must be filed at the FCA 80 business days after the ARD. They are filed electronically using the Gabriel portal.

The FCA issues regulated businesses with a schedule detailing the returns required to be filed on Gabriel and the deadlines to be applied. That schedule should be supplied to all parties involved in preparing returns and used to allocate responsibilities and agree deadlines.

## LLP tax requirements

LLP tax returns must be filed by 31 January (paper copies) or 31 October (electronic copies) as part of the self-assessment regime. Tax is paid not by the LLP, but by the members through their personal tax returns for which the same deadlines apply. Members will need to registered as self-employed and ensure they have an UTR (Unique Tax Reference number) as issued by HMRC.

## Limited company tax requirements

Limited company tax computations must be filed 12 months after the ARD but any tax due needs to be paid within nine months and one day of the year end. It is usual for the corporation tax computation to be prepared as part of the audit cycle as a limited company pays its own tax (unlike an LLP) and so the tax figure needs to be accounted for within the audited accounts. It is a Companies Act requirement that all entities keep up-to-date accounting records.

## *VAT REGISTRATION REQUIREMENT AND REPORTING*

As the majority of EU fund managers are located in the UK, this section focuses on UK VAT requirements and provides additional commentary on the general principles that also apply in other EU member states.

## VAT liability of services

In the UK the 'management' of investments and portfolios, funds, 'wrapper' products and related services, including those provided to hedge funds are a taxable service (a supply) for VAT purposes. Note that the term 'management' also includes certain activities of administering the fund as well as investment management of the assets. Any income derived from these services that would be subject to a positive VAT rate (including zero-rated) where the place of supply is in the UK (see below) is treated as being taxable income for VAT purposes.

The only exception to this relates to the management of certain collective investment undertakings available and marketed for investment by the public (this includes OEICs and Closed-ended collective investment undertakings). As the majority of hedge funds are not available to the public, and are intended for institutional investors this is unlikely to apply and is not covered here. Similarly, any intermediary services where a financial transaction takes place (separate to management services are also treated differently and can be more complex.

**Place of supply**
The place of supply of management services, and any intermediary services is determined by where the fund (client) is established. If the fund has more than one establishment, it is the establishment that is most closely connected to the services that must be looked at. VAT only needs to be charged when the fund is established in the UK. As the majority of hedge funds are established outside the UK and many will be located in non-EU jurisdictions, VAT does not have to be charged but there are special reporting requirements (see below) if the fund is located in the EU; Switzerland is not part of the EU for VAT purposes.

**VAT registration**
Once taxable income (where the place of supply is the UK) exceeds the VAT registration threshold (currently £83,000 as at June 2016) businesses are required to register for VAT. Following registration the business is required to charge VAT on any supplies that are made to any funds located in the UK. Most hedge fund managers are not required to register for VAT compulsorily as the majority (off fund

managers) tend to manage funds outside the UK, but it is advantageous to voluntarily register for VAT. There is an entitlement to reclaim any VAT incurred on business costs, including set-up costs of the business, while businesses are not required to charge any VAT as long as the funds are outside the UK or outside the EU (effectively zero rated in either case).

## VAT returns

Once registered, VAT returns must be filed quarterly, but a request may be made to submit monthly VAT returns or an annual VAT return. As most hedge fund managers receive a net repayment of VAT from HMRC it makes sense to agree shorter VAT return periods, but this is down to preference. The deadline for filing VAT returns, which must now be done electronically, is seven days and a month after the VAT return period end.

## EU reporting requirements

All businesses in EU +member states are required to report any intra-EU supplies of services between member states. Although the UK has voted for 'Brexit', the current EU VAT legislation still applies and the reporting requirements must be adhered to until further notice. EC Sales Lists must be filed for services provided to other EU member states and the period for the submissions will match the VAT return period chosen.

## Other EU businesses

The VAT liability of management services is the same in other EU member states but, as most other EU member states do not operate a VAT registration threshold, businesses are required to register for VAT as soon as trading commences. The EU reporting requirements are the same as in the UK, however the VAT return requirements differ in each EU member state. Switzerland is not part of the EU for VAT purposes, and therefore has its own separate rules.

## TAKING ON EMPLOYEES: SALARIES, TAXES AND REPORTING

**As your hedge fund manager business grows, you may need to employ staff. While this provides benefits to the owners and allows employees to focus on their areas of expertise, as a business scales it brings with it additional reporting responsibilities and other costs in addition to salaries. In this section we provide an overview of the income tax and National Insurance obligations all employers are required to fulfil.**

### PAYROLL

In the UK both income tax and National Insurance (Social Security) are collected from salaries, including bonuses, commissions and certain share equity awards, referred to as earnings, via a payroll. An employee will be subject to income tax and National Insurance based upon a number of factors, such as their residence status. Most employers will prepare their payroll using preparatory software which will enable the online reporting obligations to be made to HMRC.

Since April 2014 employers are required to operate their payroll on a real time basis, known as Real Time Information (RTI). Under RTI employers are required to ensure that certain tasks are dealt with during each pay period, for example, each month for a monthly payroll. A summary of the tasks required follows.

**Pay period responsibilities for employers**

- Record the level of earnings to be paid to each employee
- Calculate the amount of income tax and National Insurance**Error! Bookmark not defined.** to be deducted from the earnings
- Calculate the amount of employer's National Insurance due in respect of the earnings
- Produce a payslip for each employee summarising details of their earnings and deductions
- Submit a summary, known as a Full Payment Submission, detailing the earnings and deductions to HMRC
- Make payment to HMRC of the income tax and National Insurance by 19th of the following month (22nd of the following month where payments are made via BACS)

Under RTI the income tax and National Insurance must be paid across on time otherwise the employer will be liable to a late payment penalty. The penalty will be based upon the number of failures incurred during a twelve- month period, and it is intended that penalties will be issued automatically from April 2017. Note that each tax month runs from 6th of each month to 5th of the following month. The table below summarises the potential penalties due where a payment is made late.

| Late payment penalties | |
| --- | --- |
| Number of defaults in a tax year | Penalty charge applied on the amount that is paid late for the relevant month |
| First default | No penalty |
| 1 to 3 | 1% |
| 4 to 6 | 2% |
| 7 to 9 | 3% |
| 10 or more | 4% |

## Annual statement of earnings

An annual reconciliation needs to be submitted to HMRC at the end of each tax year. Employers are required to provide each employee with a summary of their earnings (P60 certificate) including details of the income tax and National Insurance deducted throughout the year. The P60 certificate must be provided to each employee by 26 May following the end of the tax year.

Employers can also use the payroll to account for tax on benefits in kind (see below) and recover other deductions from its employees, for example, employer provided loans.

## PAYE

PAYE, also known as Pay as You Earn, is the basis upon which the amount of income tax due is calculated. Income tax is generally accounted for based upon a number of factors including: monthly earnings, level of tax free earnings the employee is entitled to receive, and instructions authorised by HMRC as to the amount of tax to be deducted. Ordinarily, it is calculated on a cumulative basis throughout the tax year taking into account any entitlement to the personal allowance (£11,000 for 2016/17) before calculating the amount of tax due by reference to the prevailing tax rates.

Once an individual's income from all sources exceeds £100,000 the personal allowance is reduced by £1 for every £2 received in excess of this limit. The full benefit of the personal allowance is therefore lost once the total income exceeds £122,000 (applying 2016/17 rates).

## Application in respect of certain share equity arrangements

PAYE can also be applied to certain share equity arrangements as detailed below.

> **Circumstances where PAYE can be applied to share equity arrangements**
> - Unapproved share awards, or
> - Where there are trading arrangement in place for the purchase and sale of the shares. Commonly, this will occur where the company is listed on a recognised stock exchange or there is a special purchase vehicle, or trust in place where shares can be bought and sold, or
> - Where the company does not obtain a tax deduction for the shares it issues to its employees

Additional definitions apply to a right over a money-debt and other tradable assets not just shares. Where shares fall into one of the above categories they are referred to as 'readily convertible assets' (RCA). The employee will be required to make good the tax due on any RCA awards to the employer before 6 July (91 days) following the end of the tax year. Failure to do so will result in a secondary tax charge which is equal to the amount of the tax due on the original award. In order to prevent this secondary tax charge arising, the employer should ensure that arrangements are in place to recover the tax due from the employee. The employer will be required to pay across the tax due on the RCA on the same basis as if the employee had received their normal salary payment.

**National Insurance**

National Insurance is also calculated by reference to the employee's earnings but, unlike income tax, National Insurance is calculated based upon the employee's earnings period, for example, monthly for a monthly paid employee. The exception to this rule is in respect of a statutory director and they are subject to an annual earnings period.

Employers are also liable to National Insurance, as the secondary contributor, in respect of the salaries paid to its employees. The employer's contribution is paid to HMRC as part of the normal payroll process.

## International aspects

Consideration will need to be given to any employees who are sent on secondment to work in the UK to help start up the business for example. Where this is the case, the National Insurance treatment will vary depending upon the country of origination.

Where an employee is sent on secondment to the UK from countries within the EU/EEA or a country which holds a Social Security Reciprocal Agreement with the UK (and the relevant authorities have issued either an A1 certificate for EU/EEA countries, or a certificate of continuing coverage for reciprocal agreement countries), the employee will continue to pay Social Security contributions within their home country. Furthermore, the employer's contributions will also remain payable in the home country.

Following the result of the 'Brexit' referendum, the UK will still be considered to be an EU country for Social Security purposes until such time as the terms of the UK's exit have been negotiated.

For all other countries, often referred to as the 'Rest of the World', from where an employee is sent on secondment to the UK, no National Insurance contributions will be payable for the first 52 weeks of the assignment. Once this period has been exceeded, UK National Insurance contributions will become payable. The rules also apply in reverse, where a UK based employee is sent on secondment overseas.

The rules concerning secondees are complicated and it is recommended that advice is obtained to ensure the correct income tax and National Insurance treatment is applied to their remuneration packages.

## P11D BENEFITS IN KIND

Where an employer provides its employees with any non-cash benefits, details must be declared within a P11D, unless the item is specifically exempt and examples are provided below.

---

**Examples of benefits to be reported on a P11D include**
- Private medical insurance
- Loans in excess of £10,000
- Gym membership
- School fees
- Accommodation

---

The general rule is that the value for tax purposes of a benefit or facility made available to the employee is the cost, including VAT, regardless of whether the employer is able to recover any or all of the VAT incurred in providing the benefit. Special valuation rules apply for certain benefits.

Details of the benefit in kind will be reported on the employee's Form P11D with Class 1A National Insurance being due for payment by 19 July (22 July where payment is made via BACS) following the end of the tax year. However, where the employer is meeting a liability and the contract for the provision of those services is between the employee and the provider, the payment is a payment in kind and, therefore, subject to Class 1 National Insurance. However, where either an A1 or Continuing Certificate of Coverage is held, whereby the employee is paying Social Security in their home country, then neither Class 1/1A National Insurance will be due. Where the employer provides a mobile phone, or the use of a laptop, there will be no tax or National Insurance consequences.

The P11D will need to be submitted to HMRC on or before 6 July following the end of the tax year; a copy of the form should also be given to the employee by 6 July. Additionally, the employer is required to submit a form P11D (b), the declaration form, by 6 July.

Where P11Ds are submitted late, HMRC can seek an initial penalty of £300 and up to £60 per day for each day that a failure to make the return continues after the initial penalty is charged. Separately, where the P11D (b) is submitted late an automatic penalty of £100 per 50 employees (or part 50) for each month the form is late will be charged.

## Class 1A National Insurance

Where an employer provides any taxable benefits, an employer-only National Insurance liability will arise based upon the value of the taxable benefits provided multiplied by the relevant percentage rate applicable (currently 13.8%). The resulting Class 1A National Insurance liability is due for payment by 19 July (22 July where payment is made via BACS). However, where any employee has obtained either an A1 certificate or a Certificate of Continuing Coverage and are liable to pay Social Security contributions in their home country, then there will not be any Class 1A National Insurance liability due for the UK employer in respect of the benefits provided.

## Business expense payments exemption

From 6 April 2016, employers are required to 'self-assess' the tax and National Insurance treatment of benefits and expenses paid to employees. The practice will only be required to report any taxable benefits provided to its employees and two conditions need to be satisfied to participate.

The employer, being the payer, must operate a checking system to ensure employees are in fact incurring and claiming amounts in respect of expenses of the same kind and that a full matching deduction is provided within the legislation. In addition, neither the payer nor any person operating the checking system must know or suspect, or could reasonably be expected to know or suspect, that the employee had not incurred an amount in respect of the expense.

The checking system will require an employer to have an expense procedure in place, normally in conjunction with a staff policy. Employees must complete and submit expense claim forms detailing the reason why the expense had been incurred. Receipts must be provided as part of the claim, which will need to be reviewed and checked by a relevant individual prior to payment being made. There must be no self-authorisation of expenses.

## PAYE Settlement Agreement

Under a PAYE Settlement Agreement an employer can enter into a contract with HMRC whereby it will pay the tax and Class 1B National Insurance due on certain benefits in kind and taxable expenses under certain conditions – as set out below.

---

**Conditions for employer to pay tax and Class 1B National Insurance**
- It is impractical for the liability to be paid for by the employee
- The benefit or expense has been incurred on an irregular basis
- The benefit or taxable expense is minor in nature

---

The PAYE Settlement Agreement contract must be place before 6 July following the end of the tax year. Whilst there is no statutory deadline for the submission of the tax and Class 1B National Insurance calculation, HMRC are seeking their submission on or before 31 July, with the resulting liabilities due for payment by 19 October (22 October where payments is made via BACS).

# EMPLOYMENT TAXES: OTHER FACTORS

## Employment allowance

An allowance of £3,000 per year applies for all businesses to be offset against their Class 1 Secondary National Insurance liabilities. The allowance is claimed as part of the normal payroll process via RTI.

Where there is a group of entities, only one entity within the group can claim the £3,000 allowance. On 6 April 2016 legislation was introduced to exclude 'one man' companies from being able to claim the allowance.

## Workplace pensions

UK employers are required to provide a pension for their employees. The conditions where an employer must automatically enrol workers into a workplace pension scheme are presented below.

---

**Conditions requiring automatic enrolment into a workplace pension**
- Aged between 22 and State Pension age
- Earn more than £10,000 a year
- Work in the UK

---

Employees can opt-out of enrolment, for example if they have obtained a lifetime allowance protection certificate, or in the case of a secondee where they are participating in a pension scheme in their home country. The minimum level of pension contributions to be paid under the workplace pension regulations are set out below.

| Minimum level of pension contributions to be paid under the workplace pension regulations | | |
|---|---|---|
| Date | Employer minimum contribution | Total minimum contribution |
| Employer's staging date to 5 April 2018 | 1% | 2% (including 1% staff contribution) |
| 6 April 2018 to 5 April 2019 | 2% | 5% (including 3% staff contribution) |
| 6 April 2019 onwards | 3% | 8% (including 5% staff contribution) |

It is recommended that an Independent Financial Adviser be consulted regarding workplace pension arrangements.

*TRAVEL AND SUBSISTENCE RULES*

There are essentially two main types of journey that qualify for relief on the basis they are incurred in the performance of the duties: travel between two places of work and travel which is integral to the employment, an example of which would be journeys to visit clients/brokers/advisers.

Tax relief is not due on the cost of ordinary commuting or private travel. Consequently, this will exclude the cost of travelling between the employee's home or somewhere which is not a workplace.

**Permanent and temporary workplaces**

A workplace is defined as "a place at which the employee's attendance is necessary in the performance of their duties". The focus is on the attendance at a particular place of work as opposed to how the journey to the workplace was undertaken. HMRC have advised that there are no intentions to change the legislation in the foreseeable future. However, all travel and subsistence arrangements should be kept under regular review.

**Non-domiciled employee's travel costs**

There are additional income tax rules which need to be considered for employees who are not domiciled in the UK and are performing duties in the UK. Relief will be due in respect of the cost of a return journey home where the journey ends on, or during a period beginning within five years of the individual arriving in the UK to take up employment and the return journey is to the country where the employee normally lives. Consequently, the relief cannot be used for any other purpose.

A further relief is available which allows for the cost of the employee's spouse, including civil partners and any children, where they accompany the employee whilst they are working in the UK**Error! Bookmark not defined.**. Relief is restricted to up to two inward and two return journeys per person during each tax year.

OTHER CONSIDERATIONS

**Other considerations for the hedge fund manager start-up business owner include the following.**

*WHY OUTSOURCE YOUR FINANCE FUNCTION*

Outsourcing your hedge fund manager accounting to a specialist provider is a way to free up valuable time to focus on the tasks that matter most to your business. An internal finance function may not be required, as outsourcing teams can deliver services ranging from bookkeeping, management accounts production and VAT compliance to forecasting and preparation of statutory accounts. Alternatively, certain functions may be outsourced depending upon existing in-house expertise and availability.

## Access and value-add

With any start-up, a business owner's awareness of the financials and key performance indicators is vital to ensure the right decisions are made and quickly. Current and best in class online outsourcing solutions provide instant access to businesses' accounts from a range of devices. Online functionality includes scanning tools for invoices and receipts and also employee expense solutions with minimal inputting of data for either party. Financial information can be displayed both numerically and visually by way of graphs and charts, and can be monitored against budgets and key performance indicators.

When choosing an outsourcing provider an assessment of their sector specific credentials and knowledge should be undertaken. A sector specialist outsourcing provider will assist you with monitoring your capital requirements for regulatory compliance. It is advisable to agree in writing the scope of the services being provided, a timetable for reporting and where responsibility and accountability lies between both parties. Successful outsourcing arrangements work best where the provider focuses on building a relationship between their team and their clients, with good lines of communication, rather than just providing a bookkeeping bureau service.

## Scaleable and secure

Any solution adopted should be scaleable to grow with your business and not require significant outlay on IT software. Providers should offer multi-currency features. Finally, ensure that your provider is able to offer the necessary assurances around data security.

## CYBER SECURITY

The Cyber Essentials scheme was launched by the Government in 2014 following discussions with industry to provide a standard in cyber security relevant to all businesses sizes and sectors, from smaller SMEs, to larger not-for-profit and public-sector bodies.

It is seen as a standard which businesses can adopt and ultimately work towards certification to demonstrate to its customers and clients that cyber security is taken seriously. Business owners within the financial services sector especially may consider this of merit and taking advice from a specialist consultant on this topic is recommended.

Basic technical controls have been identified which if implemented properly could help mitigate the risks posed by unsophisticated cyber attackers. Cyber Essentials is comprised of these security controls and certification requires the implementation of all of them – and they are set out below.

---

**Cyber Essentials security controls**
- Boundary firewalls and Internet gateways – for most businesses the perimeter firewall is the first line of defence against attacks from the Internet and there are a series of best-practices which should be followed to ensure they are implemented correctly and remain effective

- Secure configuration – most computers and network devices are not considered secure upon installation (as an example using well-known passwords for administrator accounts) and a series of steps are usually necessary to provide a secure environment

- User access control – administrator accounts usually have the greatest level of access to data, applications and computers within an IT system. To protect against the unauthorised use of

---

them requires effective access control management, such as the use of password controls and the principle of least privilege

- Malware protection – computers (and systems) exposed to the Internet should be protected against malware (a term which includes viruses, worms and spyware) which can be introduced into an IT system via web browsing, receiving emails and opening attachments from USB memory devices. Businesses should therefore ensure they have effective technical controls in place to reduce these risks

- Patch management – computers and network devices/appliances typically run software which may contain vulnerabilities. These can sometimes be exploited by malicious individuals to attack a business's IT system. The major vendors work hard to discover these vulnerabilities and then release patches to fix them. Businesses should ensure that processes are in place to manage the patching process.

# S2. Selecting an Accountancy Firm/Auditor, including suggested key questions

## Choosing your auditor

Again, 'soft' issues may well come to the fore when selecting an auditor. As when choosing any service provider, cultural fit is key and, at the most basic level, one would hope both parties will get on. While business owners and auditors do not need to live in each other's pockets, a good line of communication is vital and this becomes critical if a transaction is undertaken. Business owners should ask themselves whether they would be happy taking advice from a prospective auditor.

An internal finance team if there is one should also be able to work effectively with the auditor.

## Credentials

For businesses operating in the financial services arena, weight should be allocated to an auditor's sector specialism, given the specific requirements of the regulatory framework in which they operate. Recommendations are helpful and references are a prerequisite. While a transaction may seem a long way off, consider up front the other services you may require such as outsourced accounting, tax compliance, company secretarial, VAT and payroll services. There can be considerable benefits and cost savings to be had from using one supplier for all service lines where this is possible.

## Quality and cost savings

Many hedge fund managers are not aware that the auditor for the hedge fund business and that of the fund do not have to be one and the same. The division of these services between two auditors can deliver a better level of service (we don't mind being kept on our toes by healthy competition) and further cost savings, especially if you split the fund and the fund manager business audits between large and say, mid-tier firms. It should be recognised that while big firms may specialise in fund audits, the size of the hedge fund business audit may not secure the same level of attention or quality of service from a large firm as it might from a smaller firm.

Consider carefully the terms of engagement and the terms of business that your chosen auditor offers before signing on the dotted line. It is not unreasonable to request a three year fee forecast based on your budgets, continuity of service team and agree a timetable for your audit upfront. When doing so, make sure key deadlines and responsibilities of both parties are clear so that nothing is left until the last minute – this will ensure filing deadlines are made with time to spare and that a good relationship is maintained.

Hedge fund managers typically get 80 business days from their year-end to file accounts with the FCA. In order for this deadline to be met, an appropriate planning process and an agreed timetable must be in place.

## WHAT MAKES HAYSMACINTYRE THE ACCOUNTANCY/AUDITING FIRM OF CHOICE?

haysmacintyre is a single office firm of Chartered Accountants based in Holborn, central London, comprising 32 partners and over 200 staff. We are among only a few firms which bridge the gap between the larger firms which do everything but can lack the personal touch and smaller firms which are only able to provide a narrow range of services.

Our established Financial Services sector team includes over 100 fund managers in its client portfolio. Our expert staff, who receive specialised training, have been working with fund managers and their businesses for over fifteen years.

haysmacintyre's unique blank page audit approach, eAudit, requires every audit to be tailored to each client's specific needs to achieve the most robust and best value audit service for clients. Our client knowledge and ethos of wanting to help our clients succeed in business drives our investment in client-facing time and continuity of service – and this delivers both a quality service and savings to our clients – principles that influence all of our teams.

We are proud that our audit approach and client focused ethos has driven our audit practice to be substantially larger than many bigger firms. Our audit client profile, includes numerous listed and public interest bodies and is exceptional for a mid-size firm. Our tax department also has the expertise to advise on all Corporation Tax, Employment Tax and VAT requirements.

> "We are among only a few firms which bridge the gap between the larger firms which do everything but can lack the personal touch and smaller firms which are only able to provide a narrow range of services."

haysmacintyre is the joint owner and a member firm of MSI Global Alliance (MSI), which comprises over 250 independent legal and accounting firms operating locally in 100 countries around the world. Through our alliance, we can deliver high quality and local accounting and legal services worldwide.

haysmacintyre was named Mid-Tier Firm of the Year at The British Accountancy Awards in 2014. This award recognises our client service, quality of our delivery, people, innovation and commitment to the sectors we service. In the 2016 awards, haysmacintyre was a finalist in the 'top 50 audit team of the year' category.

## KEY QUESTIONS TO ASK YOUR POTENTIAL ACCOUNTANT/AUDITOR

How will you communicate with me as your client? And how often should I expect to hear from you during and outside of the audit period?

How will you work with my in-house finance team?

Is there a charge for any ad hoc email or telephone enquiries I might have; when can I expect the 'clock to start running'?

What are your fees and billing schedules?

What are your sector specialisms; what is your experience of working with Financial Services businesses?

How familiar are you with the specific regulations that apply to financial services businesses?

What financial services businesses do you have in your client portfolio and what transactions if any have your supported them through?

Who will you provide as a reference?

What other services do you offer – and can I outsource my accounting to you?

## CONTACT INFORMATION

**Primary Contact:** Bernadette King

bking@haysmacintyre.com

+44 20 7969 5544

**Alternative Contact:** Melanie Pittas

mpittas@haysmacintyre.com

+44 20 7969 5621

Switchboard: +44 20 7969 5500

**Website:** www.haysmacintyre.com

**Address:** 26 Red Lion Square, London WC1R 4AG

# CHAPTER 6. FUND ADMINISTRATION FOR EUROPEAN HEDGE FUNDS

By Peter Jakubicka of Circle Partners

## About the author

*Peter Jakubicka, LL.M. is the Business Development Manager of Circle Partners based in the Netherlands, having joined the group in May of 2012. Circle Partners is a worldwide niche service provider having expanded from its origins in the Netherlands, it now occupies a global position, with offices in Hong Kong, the Netherlands, Luxembourg, Orlando, British Virgin Islands, Cayman Islands, Curacao, Switzerland and the Slovak Republic and beyond with its network of strategic international partners. Before joining Circle Partners, Peter was a legal counsel of Aegon, a worldwide insurance and pension asset management company headquartered in the Netherlands. He has over a decade's experience in the alternative investment market, asset management sector. Peter trained and qualified as a lawyer and holds two master degrees.*

## About Circle Partners

Circle Partners is an independent fund administrator specialised in rendering accounting and administration, shareholder and organisational services to investment funds established in a different number of jurisdictions and with diverse investment strategies. Our goal is to assist asset managers in building their investment fund and enabling them to concentrate on the asset management business through a process of outsourcing virtually all back-office functions to Circle Partners. Special care and attention is given to accurate and swift communication with the fund manager and shareholders to enhance client satisfaction and confidence and to assist in creating a sound reputation for the fund.

## PART 1 – INTRODUCTION

The essential party of every established Hedge Fund is the administrator. What is the role of the Hedge Fund administrator ("HFA")? What does the HFA do? What is the importance of Hedge Fund administration?

The industry environment, particularly in the sheer number of Hedge Funds across the globe, creates a challenging environment for the establishment of a successful hedge fund. A necessary element for growth and development is the HFA that takes care of the administration of hedge funds and their basic day-to-day operations.

Generally, the HFA is responsible for ensuring the efficient operations of a hedge fund, whilst at the same time relieving the investment manager from the necessary subsidiary tasks. A good hedge fund administrator can relieve a significant amount of the burden from the manager and improve the consistency with which certain tasks are handled. Many managers use HFAs to serve their investors and

> "A good hedge fund administrator can relieve a significant amount of the burden from the manager and improve the consistency with which certain tasks are handled"

106

effectively act as their outsourced accounting department.

Typical services provided are independent monthly accounting and net asset value (NAV) calculations, performance fee calculations, record keeping of investors and management fee calculations, legal support and communication with the shareholders. While these functions can certainly be done internally, it can be time consuming for the manager to do them and costly if staff is hired to perform them - particularly in the early stages of a hedge fund.

Apart from the aforementioned duties, HFA may also be responsible for ensuring that a hedge fund complies with the terms of its Offering Memorandum /or/ Prospectus /or/ PPM, including the management of its investment portfolio with regards to investment restrictions and diversification requirements.

## PART 2 – ESTABLISHMENT OF A HEDGE FUND

Many hedge fund managers retain legal advisers who can advise in relation to the set up and establishment of future hedge funds. Multiple law firms may be required depending on the particular construction of a particular hedge fund.

However, some HFAs take a more proactive role than others in the hedge fund establishment process, helping to draft the documents, liaising with lawyers in the jurisdiction selected and generally acting as "project manager". Hedge Fund managers establishing a hedge fund in a jurisdiction for the first time will clearly have a number of questions ranging from complex operational points to regulatory issues, where applicable. A hedge fund manager can often obtain useful advice and guidance from the HFA regarding the establishment and ongoing operations of a hedge fund in the desired jurisdiction.

Many hedge fund managers select fund lawyers as a first step, with the choice of HFA often being made at a much later stage. However, there are benefits in choosing the HFA early on in the process as it enables the lawyers and the HFA to liaise in relation to operational aspects of the Hedge Fund structure at the outset, thereby avoiding any practical difficulties that may arise at a later point in the establishment process. Moreover, many HFAs can provide sufficient and quality law services in order to avoid further expenses on the third-party law firms (say, in regard to legal advice related to the jurisdiction of the fund).

The Hedge Fund Administrator may be able to provide useful guidance on various areas in respect of the Hedge Fund which have an operational impact, although it is not its role or responsibility to provide legal or regulatory advice. Typically, the areas in which the HFA may assist will include regulatory requirements (if applicable, e.g., compliance with the EU Savings Tax Directive, FATCA and CRS), interaction with investment managers and/or prime brokers, fee structures (in particular, performance fees and equalization measures), law services, shareholder communication, currency class hedging, AML reviews and subscription, transfer and redemption procedures among others.

Both the HFA and lawyers have practical experience of the length of time it will take to establish a hedge fund in the relevant jurisdiction and the volume of documentation required. They will, therefore, be well placed to give a hedge fund manager a realistic view of the timeframe within which it can reasonably expect to be operating from that jurisdiction. Clearly, the timeframe within which a Hedge Fund can be established will vary greatly between jurisdictions, particularly if the Hedge Fund and, in some cases, the manager undergo an authorization or approval process by the regulator in that particular jurisdiction.

An essential for every hedge fund is a Prospectus. The investment manager and the Hedge Fund's directors must ensure that the prospectus is accurate and discloses all relevant information, including the role of the HFA, relevant provisions of the HFA's agreement, valuation provisions and subscription/redemption procedures. The HFA will review the operational aspects of the prospectus of a hedge fund, in detail, prior to launch. It is essential that all operational and practical aspects of a hedge fund are correctly reflected in the prospectus as the HFA will rely on the terms of the prospectus in operating a hedge fund on an ongoing basis. Furthermore, it is important that the prospectus comprehensively describes the manner in which the HFA will perform its duties. While the prospectus is the formal responsibility of the board of directors, all parties should review the Prospectus and ensure that it accurately and appropriately reflects how a hedge fund will be managed, administered and operated as relevant to each party.

In furtherance, the enclosure of the administration agreement is necessary in order to establish the relationship between a fund and the HFA. This agreement will specifically describe all of the duties which have to be undertaken by the HFA in its capacity as administrator of a hedge fund. It is important for both parties to clearly and sufficiently express the manner in which these functions will be undertaken. Administration agreements are frequently accompanied by the SLAs which reflect in more detail how the HFA will interact on a daily basis with a hedge fund, the investment manager and investors.

The Administrator is the contact point for investors to subscribe capital – they will be able to inform the manager of flows and cleared funds. Often the AML requirements are met by processes conducted by the HFA.

SLAs are not typically legally binding; they generally describe an operational, escalation and communication framework under which it is envisaged that a hedge fund, the HFA and other service providers will operate.

The legal agreement, for e.g. the administration agreement which a fund will enter into with the HFA, should set out the contractual arrangements between a fund and the HFA. These agreements would not normally describe the individual steps that each party should undertake in performing its obligations under the relevant contract, nor would they describe, in detail, how the parties will work together. For this reason, the administration agreement is generally supplemented by a Service Level agreement (SLA).

The SLA basically lays out the detailed operational responsibilities, duties and expectations in plain language and should present measurable objectives for all parties. The intention is to provide a background for how the Hedge Fund will be managed and administered and how the parties intend to interact. It is usually a living document which is likely to evolve over time.

For example, a SLA might indicate a detailed timeline for the communication and processing of trade instructions from execution of the deal at the Hedge Fund manager to their incorporation in the books and records. Hedge Funds and HFAs will agree on the level of detail and the degree to which the SLA is intended to be prescriptive or guidance in nature. For example, the SLA might contain a clause that the NAV will be sent by the HFA so-many-days after month-end, though on a best endeavours basis. While every SLA will differ, the overriding objective of each one is to ensure that the Hedge Fund administration process is documented, achievable and will result in a satisfactory administration service being delivered.

## PART 3 - ADMINISTRATION OF A HEDGE FUND

One of the most important tasks of a HFA is the calculation of the NAV. In a nutshell, the NAV is the price at which the potential shareholders buy and sell the shares of the Hedge Fund. It is also the key determinant in reporting Hedge Fund performance, calculating fees and producing financial reports. The accurate and timely calculation of the NAV is therefore a vital and repeated process. The process of the NAV calculation consists of five main steps: trade capture, security valuation, reconciliations, expense calculation and holding current authorized signatory list of investors.


**Trade Capture**

There are two basic types of transactions that the HFA needs to process in the books and records – transactions reflecting investor activity and the transactions reflecting trading activity. Due to the fact that Hedge Funds only allow subscriptions and redemptions on a monthly or quarterly basis and tend to be aimed at high net worth or institutional investors, the investors' activity tends to be less voluminous in comparison with other types of investment funds. Even a large hedge fund can have only a couple of dozen investors. However, an efficient communication is required between the investor dealing teams and the valuation teams to ensure that the valuation system is updated for all investor dealing. Most HFAs will have an electronic link between the investor dealing system and the valuation system. In some administration companies, these two functions may be combined.

The level of portfolio trading activity varies between hedge funds, depending on the strategy the each particular hedge fund is pursuing. It is essential that the trading activity of a fund is properly reflected in the valuation systems of the HFA. Most hedge funds and prime brokers have the capability to communicate electronically trade files on a daily basis, detailing all the trades done. The method of communication will differ, depending on the technological sophistication of the manager, but electronic communication is usually the most efficient way of communication. Other methods include SWIFT, FTP or CSV/Excel files that are pushed to the HFA.

Once received, the HFA will process the transaction activity into the books and records. For many asset types, most HFAs will have the capability to upload these trade details in an automated fashion. Some asset types, especially various exotic over the counter ("OTC") instruments may require manual intervention. To ensure independence of record keeping the HFA should receive all trades from the investment manager and then reconcile all transactions with the relevant prime broker, counterparty or custodian. The manager's own systems and processes will agree trade blotters with the PB, and operations staff then spend time on any trade differences. Often the trades sent to the HFA have been agreed with the PB already.

**Security Valuation**

There are two main aspects to the valuation process - price collection and price governance. Price collection covers the mechanical process of collecting prices from agreed sources at agreed times. Price governance covers the process by which the pricing policy, controls, responsibilities, disputes and issues are escalated and resolved. Accepted international sound practice provides for the establishment of a pricing committee and the creation of a pricing policy document. The price collection process should then be documented in the pricing policy document and should provide for pricing sources, cut off times etc., as well as for escalation procedures, approvals, tolerances, manual processing and hierarchies (if applicable).

In all cases, it is important to consider the independence of the pricing process. Wherever possible, but subject in all cases to a hedge fund's pricing policy, the HFA should seek independent sources for the valuation of the assets of a hedge fund. However, there will be occasions when valuations of certain instruments can only be made by the manager and the issuer of the instrument, or by the manager alone. In these cases, it is important that the method of valuation is documented, checked where a secondary source is available and reported to the pricing committee or board, periodically.

Particular consideration should be given to OTC or unquoted instruments, for e.g. securities that are not quoted that may be highly illiquid and difficult to value accurately. Considerations include whether counterparty valuations are available and/or appropriate and whether the instruments can be valued by independent vendors. The pricing policy document will provide clarity on the relative priority of sources and tolerances between various sources available. It should also be noted that certain jurisdictions place greater reliance on a counterparty price and any specific jurisdictional requirements need to be reflected in the pricing policy. The pricing policy document should be approved by the board or governing body of the Hedge Fund on a regular basis (annually or when altered).

It should be noted that while some HFAs have people, teams and service models which are capable of, and expert in, the calculation of recommended prices for individual securities, many others are not. A hedge fund manager or investor should not automatically assume that the HFA offers this service, employs this expertise or takes this responsibility. For this reason not all HFAs will work with all hedge fund investment strategies. Even where the investment strategy only involves Listed instruments the HFA may ask to cover higher expenses with higher fees for high turnover systematic strategies.

**Reconciliations**

In calculating a reliable NAV, a thorough and complete reconciliation of cash and trading positions to the prime broker and other brokers needs to be carried out on a traded and settled basis (although a settled and traded reconciliation may not always be possible). All assets held by a fund should be reconciled between the HFA's records and those of the relevant third parties. This will include assets or collateral held with prime brokers, futures brokers, CFD counterparties, OTC counterparties, custodians or any other group, with all material differences and breaks understood and documented prior to NAV determination.

The reconciliations should encompass nominal holdings, value and transactions entered into during the period. The HFA should normally be able to show that the prime broker is reflecting the same trades, holding the same positions and valuing those positions in line with the HFA's own records and that any break can be explained satisfactorily. Some HFAs may offer a three-way reconciliation facility where the books of the HFA, prime broker and Hedge Fund manager are reconciled periodically.

**Expense Calculation**

A hedge fund must accrue its expenses accurately and on a timely basis in order to strike an accurate NAV. All known variable and fixed fees including administration, management, performance, custody, audit fees, legal expenses, listing expenses and directorship fees need to be accrued. Many hedge funds and HFAs will agree an expense budget or schedule in advance of hedge fund's launch to govern the accrual process. The annual budget should be agreed with the client at the start of each fiscal year. Of these expenses, potentially the most complex fee is the performance fee, which can be calculated using multiple different methods. It should be noted that some regulators require sight of the performance fee wording and a worked example in order to approve a hedge fund.

## NAV Calculation and Reporting

The final step in calculating the NAV of a fund is to calculate the NAV per share of each class in issue. In order to do this, the HFA will typically do the following:

(i) calculate the allocation ratio for each class in issue (some of the classes can be a founders' class which attracts no management and performance fees);

(ii) allocate the income, expenses, gains and losses for a hedge fund based on the above allocation ratio;

(iii) adjust for any share class specific items, such as any hedging gain/loss, new issue profits, differing management and performance fees;

(iv) calculate the NAV per share;

(v) agree the NAV with a Fund's manager; and

(vi) distribute the NAV.

In addition, there may be a set of variables which may require additional processing or consideration including: multi class/multi currency processing and hedging (for e.g. where classes of shares are issued in a currency other than the base currency), the fact that some fees may be deferred or reinvested and any such arrangement will require processing, some hedge funds may offer shares at a discount or premium, arising from fees or charges; and if a Hedge Fund is subject to adverse or unusual market conditions, additional market or valuation provisions may be required. The base currency would usually be in $ or € depending on the larger class on Day One. The base currency is the one in which the books and records of the fund are denominated, and normally align with the currency denomination of the portfolio management system of the Manager.

Many hedge funds agree to a process up front of launch where the NAV is subject to a review by the Hedge Fund manager in advance of its release to investors. Such review is generally an additional control which assists in ensuring that the records are reconciled with those of the Hedge Fund manager. It is not intended to replace any control within the HFA and is not intended to absolve the HFA from agreed and documented contractual responsibility.


## PART 4 – ADDITIONAL ADMINISTRATION SERVICES


It is the primary job of the HFA to calculate a hedge fund's NAV and deal with its investors but, it may well be the case that the GFA offers other services. A number of these services named within this part is not definite and terminal. There may be other services regularly employed by HFAs but the intention of this section is to describe the more common aspects of the HFA service and provides for some discussion of sound practice in these areas. It should be noted that the provision of the services below may, by definition, require a different contractual appointment, e.g., the appointment of a bank, FX counterparty or custodian.


### Middle Office Services

Outside of the core NAV calculation role a hedge fund might choose to outsource middle office functions to its HFA. Many of these services provided by HFAs were traditionally performed by the operations and finance teams of the investment manager. It should be noted that while many HFAs offer this service, many others do not. A Fund and its investment manager need to understand the HFA's capabilities in this area, should a middle office service be of interest.

By Middle Office Services are meant services provided by HFAs on a daily basis which typically consist of trade capture and confirmation procedures; corporate action procedures; cash; trade and position reconciliations; portfolio profit and loss calculation; and analysis and detailed portfolio reporting. They also can incorporate, and not necessarily on a daily basis, collateral management; cash balance management; risk management; performance measurement; pricing procedures and technology services, including maintenance of the applicable technology and more. When deciding on an operating model, a hedge fund should not just research the services that HFAs can offer, but determine what services a hedge fund is willing for the HFA to exert more control over.

The decision to outsource operational functions for a start-up hedge fund is typically arrived at after the senior appointments have been made within the start-up management firm. As the functions outsourced will have a critical impact on the daily running of a hedge fund, it is important that the senior management agree on the services that they are comfortable with the HFA performing. In addition, a full understanding of how these services will be provided by the HFA is important. Making the decision to outsource middle office functions prior to having a hedge fund COO or CFO in place might lead to uncertainty at a later stage, in terms of how the Hedge Fund will operate, and some of the advantages of outsourcing may be lost.

To effectively manage outsourced services, such as those listed above, the HFA will require technology to efficiently capture, process and store trading activity. Technology capable of storing and processing data required for operational processes, valuation and portfolio analysis such as yield curves, security static or corporate action information forms the basis of any outsourced solution.

Many HFAs will provide daily portfolio accounting and performance as part of a middle office solution. This service requires the HFA's technology to be advanced enough to capture and present all relevant data to perform the portfolio calculations required for this function. The

HFA's technology will be often able to support the viewing of near real time profit and loss information for each position held by a hedge fund. A fund may make the decision that the trade capture and portfolio technology employed by the HFA to provide such services is sufficiently powerful to adequately support the operating model chosen for a fund. In this instance, a fund avoids incurring the additional overhead costs of separate order and portfolio management systems. The decision on out-sourcing in these regards is often taken based on the basis of a combination of the business model of the Manager and the investment strategy undertaken. It is unlikely that an investment strategy based on complex instruments would be suitable to view through an outsourced portfolio management system.

Dependent on what is to be outsourced, a clear operating model has to be established and understood by the Hedge Fund and the HFA. The sections of the operating model outsourced to the HFA and the SLA that supports it becomes the product a fund has invested in. Over time, this product will need to develop as a hedge fund's assets expand and as additional products and complexity are added. Therefore, when choosing a service provider to outsource functions to, the Hedge Fund should look at the scalability that the HFA offers, both in terms of technology and staff expertise. A hedge fund must then decide if the HFA has the ability to support the operating model agreed, given potential expansion in the future.

The middle office services provided by the HFA will generally require that any SLA or equivalent document between the two parties be more detailed than a situation where only back office services are provided. An additional level of operational risk is introduced if there is not a complete understanding of a fund's operating model, across both organizations. This understanding of the SLA is also part of ensuring a successful relationship between the two organizations which becomes increasingly important when outsourcing functions.

# PART 5 – TAX SERVICES OF THE HEDGE FUND ADMINISTRATOR

Many hedge funds seek to attract US investors (both taxable and non-taxable) to invest in their Hedge Funds. If they do, this may give rise to a requirement for US tax reporting requirements. HFAs will therefore need to have staff and systems to produce the often intricate information required for US tax reporting or be in touch with US tax advisors. In addition, the HFA should be able to identify when a tax decision has to be made and alert the relevant tax decision makers, while not taking responsibility for the tax decision. In that case, the HFA needs to have an understanding of the tax reporting requirements, as well as the systems and staff to support these requirements.

**FATCA services**

The Foreign Account Tax Compliance Act (FATCA) is a US Law which has taken effect on 1 January, 2013. The primary goal of this legislation is to identify assets held and income earned by U.S. citizens from offshore sources to ensure that the relevant taxes have been assessed and paid. Foreign Financial Institutions ("FFIs") which do not comply with such rules are subject to withholding tax of 30% on U.S. sourced income. FATCA is complex legislation which is deemed to have a dramatic and wide sweeping impact on non-U.S. financial institutions, including banks, custodians, offshore Hedge Funds, insurance companies and trusts. We will hereby outline the impact on the offshore Hedge Funds industry, specifically the role of HFA in the implementation and ongoing compliance with FATCA.

Broadly, FATCA applies to any FFI which has either U.S. investors, or receives U.S. sourced income. The definition of FFI covers the majority of funds, including mutual funds, funds of funds, exchange-traded funds, private equity and venture capital funds, other managed funds,

119

commodity pools and Hedge Funds. The fund entity itself is considered as the FFI.

If a Hedge Fund doesn't cooperate and complies with FATCA, it is at risk of incurring a 30% withholding tax on all proceeds from its direct or indirect investment in U.S. assets. For many established offshore Hedge Funds, the initial implementation was costly and complicated. Collecting, verifying and managing data, as well as performing U.S. tax reporting and possibly withholding, lead to large upfront costs for enhancing or implementing new systems, processes and training. Depending on the due diligence policies of the Hedge Fund, some investors, U.S. and foreign, now need to provide additional documentation when subscribing to a Hedge Fund.

In light of FATCA regulations, Hedge Funds are deemed as FFI and have to fulfill several requirements, such as: appointment of a FATCA Reporting Officer, adopting written policies and procedures to govern the due diligence process, obtaining information on account holders to determine which are U.S. and non-U.S. persons, recalcitrant and non-participating FFI ("NPFFI") persons, reporting to the Internal Revenue Service ("IRS") on U.S. and recalcitrant accounts, withholding on payments made to NPFFIs and recalcitrant account holders as of 2014 and certifying compliance to the IRS. HFAs provide FATCA services to the Hedge Funds as a part of the administration agreements enclosed with the Hedge Funds.

### FATCA - Due Diligence requirements

U.S. based Hedge Funds' FATCA responsibilities extend beyond just "submitting the forms." A Hedge Fund must perform specified due diligence to validate its withholding certificates to avoid potential liability for tax, interest and penalties resulting from the failure to perform FATCA withholding. Following is a brief overview of some of these procedures.

A U.S. - based Hedge Fund receiving a Form W-8 must review whether the certificate is incomplete or contains information that is inconsistent with the investor's claims, whether the Hedge Fund has other account information that conflicts with the investor's claims, and whether the withholding certificate lacks information necessary to establish entitlement to an exemption from FATCA withholding. In other words, Hedge Funds must know the forms (including countless defined terms) so they can assess whether they are filled out correctly, and must cross-check other information maintained by the Hedge Fund against the forms.

If an investor claims foreign status (e.g., by proving a Form W-8BEN or W-8BEN-E), then except in certain cases in which a GIIN is provided, the Hedge Fund must scrub its files for specified U.S. indicia (such as a U.S. address) and, if necessary, obtain follow-up information to establish foreign status. A withholding agent must also confirm that a GIIN is provided if required, and that the GIIN and investor's name appear on the IRS website within 90 days. If an investor provides a GIIN, the Hedge Fund must also confirm, at least annually, that the GIIN has not been removed from the IRS list. Additional due diligence may be required depending on the particular type of FATCA status claimed, and relaxed due diligence procedures are available for certain preexisting obligations (investors).

**Financial Statements**

Hedge Funds usually produce two sets of financial statements each year, comprising audited annual financial statements and unaudited semi-annual financial statements. The board or general partner is generally responsible for the preparation of the financial statements, although the role of formally compiling the accounts is usually delegated to the HFA, with key inputs and advice from the investment manager and auditor, where appropriate. Where funds are established as investment companies, the company law provisions of the relevant

121

jurisdiction will invariably require that an audited set of accounts be prepared in respect of the preceding financial year. Similar requirements (whether legislative or regulatory) are generally imposed on non-corporate fund vehicles such as unit trusts and limited partnerships. While some jurisdictions do not require a Hedge Fund to produce semi-annual financial statements, very often listing requirements or investor expectations will dictate that such statements are produced.

The content of financial statements will vary from jurisdiction to jurisdiction but, at a minimum, both sets of financial statements will include a profit and loss account, balance sheet and commentary from the fund manager on the performance of the Hedge Fund for the period under review. The annual audited financial statements will also include an auditor's report. Both the International Accounting Standards Board (IASB) and Financial Accounting Standards Board (FASB) are continuously updating standards which may have a significant impact on the financial statements of an investment fund. HFAs must consistently upgrade and enhance their IT infrastructure and reporting capabilities to ensure synchronicity with the latest requirements.

The HFA's role in producing both sets of financial statements is central. There must be adequate mapping of balances from the HFA's systems to the financial statements and data collection for certain disclosures. For the annual statements, the HFA will liaise with the auditors to ensure that the audit review is conducted on an orderly basis and that all queries are addressed in a timely manner. Semi-annual financial statements might be prepared by the HFA without referral to the Hedge Fund's auditors, who would not be expected to issue a report on such statements. Auditors are hardly ever involved at the half year stage. The HFA may facilitate the filing of financial statements with the relevant authorities within the required deadlines, depending on the Hedge Fund structure, regulatory guidelines and service levels agreed.

# PART 6 - ADDITIONAL ADMINISTRATION POSSIBILITIES

The Hedge Fund administration industry encompasses service providers with widely differing business models, ranging from the institutional structure of custodian banks to the more boutique nature of niche service providers. As a consequence, HFAs approach the area of client relationship management in very different ways. Some groups have dedicated relationship managers whilst others see relationship management as an extension of the operational staffs' core responsibilities.

Majority of jurisdictions requires that Hedge Funds established as corporate vehicles must appoint a company secretary. Number of the company secretarial duties, in particular those duties relating to shareholder services, tend to overlap with certain of the HFA's duties. Since the HFA, rather than the company secretary, maintains and updates the share register of the Hedge Fund, the former is the primary point of contact for the shareholders. Therefore, some HFAs are well placed to provide company secretarial services to corporate Hedge Fund vehicles, whether as company secretary of record or at a practical level only, with a director or other person/entity being named as the secretary of record.

The duties of a company secretary consists of: organization and complex support of board meetings, general meetings, extraordinary meetings, statutory registers, share registration, shareholder communications, company seal, registered office authentication of documents of the company and many others.

## Part 7 - What Makes Circle Partners the Fund Administrators of Choice?

Circle Partners is particularly good at delivering tailor made solutions to its clients and providing turn-key solutions. Starting from an initial advice given to clients on structuring possibilities and continuing with first class administration services delivered. Circle Partners has seasoned staff with years of experience and clients appreciate a low turnover of key personnel.

## Key Questions to Ask Your Potential Fund Administrator

What is in your standard Service Level Agreement?

How committed are you to future technology developments/spending?

What are your fee models?

Do you have metrics for the stability of your team?

To what extent are you able to act as a project manager in the launch phase? How are you compensated for this work?

What input can you provide on the fee terms that are currently commercial – what is high/low or attractive to investors?

Will you help to choose the right structure for my hedge fund?

Do you have good banking relationships that I could make use of?

Do you have good brokerage relationships that I could make use of?

Do you have experience with my strategy?

## CONTACT INFORMATION

Circle Investment Support Services B.V.

**Primary Contact:** Gerben Oldekamp, Managing director

+31 33 467 3880

goldekamp@circlepartners.com

**Alternative contact:** Peter Jakubicka, Business Development Manager

pjakubicka@circlepartners.com

Switchboard: +31 33 467 3880

**Website:** www.circlepartners.com

**Address:** Smallepad 30F, 3811 MG Amersfoort, The Netherlands

Circle Partners has offices in AMERSFOORT, BRATISLAVA, BVI, CAYMAN, CURACAO, HONG KONG, LUXEMBOURG, ORLANDO, and ZURICH

# Chapter 7. Prime Brokerage For European Hedge Funds

By James Skeggs of Societe Generale Prime Services

## About the author

*James Skeggs is the Global Head of Alternative Investment Consulting at Societe Generale Prime Services with responsibilities for the development of investor focused market commentary on a wide variety of hedge fund strategies. James has written extensively on the performance characteristics of managed futures, global macro, commodity, and volatility strategies, as well as various portfolio and index construction questions. He is Chairman of the group's Index Committee, spearheaded the launch of a number of strategy indices, and has designed customised performance and risk reporting for managed account investors. He is a regular participant at industry conferences and events, and is frequently published or quoted in journals and media. In 2014 he was listed as one of the Rising Stars of Trading and Technology by Financial News. James holds a BSc (Hons) in Chemistry from Durham University, is a CAIA designee, and worked for Ruffer LLP prior to joining Fimat in 2004.*

## About Societe Generale Prime Services

Societe Generale Prime Services part of the Global Markets' division of Societe Generale Corporate & Investment Banking is the bank's prime brokerage business, offering a unique combination of execution, clearing, custody and financing services. It is truly multi-asset and multi-instrument across Listed Derivatives, Equities (Cash/synthetic), FX, Fixed Income and OTC Cleared. As a firm offering world leading derivatives brokerage services, unrivalled access to 125+ markets and exchange venues, Societe Generale Prime services provides its clients an extensive pool of liquidity and tailored value added services.

## PART 1 – INTRODUCTION

As the term "Hedge Fund" covers such a diverse range of investment strategies, there is a wide variety of requirements placed upon an investment bank by its hedge fund clients. Prime brokerage is the term used to describe all these various services and the relationship between a hedge fund and its prime broker(s) is – more than any other counterparty - of paramount importance to the success of a hedge fund.

The core prime brokerage services include the execution, clearing, settlement, and custody of all trades/positions of a hedge fund in addition to acting as a key financing counterparty. Each prime broker will have different capabilities in these core areas and will likely offer numerous additional services in addition to these core services in order to differentiate themselves in an increasingly commoditised market.

This chapter will look to describe the relationship between a hedge fund and its prime broker, and detail the various prime brokerage services for securities and derivatives, in addition to the operational support and other services offered.

# PART 2 – THE PRIME BROKER-HEDGE FUND RELATIONSHIP

The relationship with its prime broker is of critical importance to a hedge fund, and the key to a successful partnership is the ability of the entire prime brokerage organisation to understand the investment strategy of the hedge fund and anticipate their needs as they develop. Equally, it must be able to grow with the fund to ensure that it has access to the full range of services required. In short, the prime broker has become more of a business partner to hedge funds than ever before, providing mission critical advice to help them succeed.

A prime brokerage team typically encompasses a number of different roles and a successful, prime broker-hedge fund partnership relies on strong working relationships at all levels in both organisations. Hedge funds should expect to maintain a regular dialogue with their prime broker's sales, relationship management, client services, risk, capital introduction, consulting, trade execution and financing teams. These relationships should be evaluated on a frequent basis to ensure that they are working effectively.

Given the central role prime brokers play, the selection of a primer broker is a critical decision that hedge fund managers need to manage carefully, The first step in this process is to ensure that a hedge fund identifies the services they are likely to require from their prime broker and which way they will prioritise those services.  As a hedge fund grows they may find that there are specific requirements which cannot be fulfilled by their existing prime broker, or face calls from investors to diversify their counterparties. At this point a hedge fund should look to add additional prime brokers and identify a counterpart that is complementary to their existing setup, bearing in mind the balances or volumes they may be able to provide to their new counterparty.

Prime brokers have been significantly impacted by the raft of regulatory changes that have unfolded in recent years, especially increased demands for greater transparency, oversight, and regulation. Many of these changes have already affected the relationships between hedge funds and their prime brokers, and will continue to do so due to changes in the financing model of the prime brokerage itself. Scarce resource management is at the forefront of the running of a prime brokerage business, with a bright spotlight being shone on a raft of new balance sheet metrics driven by Basel III and bank solvency regulations. These new metrics, , mean that prime brokers must re-evaluate the ways in which they determine the value of a relationship with a hedge fund, and hedge fund managers need in turn to understand these changes. The ability to assist clients in navigating a complex and still evolving space will be key to many funds.

## PART 3 – SECURITIES PRIME BROKERAGE

The typical definition of a hedge fund strategy is an investment fund that employs leverage and hedges exposure through shorting. This section focuses on the dedicated services that are provided to hedge funds for tradable financial assets such as equity and debt securities.

### Long Book Financing (Leverage Provision)

A hedge fund that wishes to purchase equity or debt securities in excess of their total assets requires additional capital, and the provision of this financing is one of the key roles of a prime broker. The amount of financing available to a hedge fund will be a function of the collateral (assets) that the hedge fund is able to post with the prime broker in addition to the risk management methodology, and balance sheet constraints of the prime broker. More financing will typically be extended to funds with liquid and diversified portfolios; whilst illiquid or concentrated portfolios will experience greater haircuts, which will limit the amount of financing that may be extended.

In addition to the amount of financing available, fund managers need to think about the expected duration of financing. Committed or term financing may be available from the prime broker, though there will certainly be cost implications (particularly due to regulatory changes such as Basel III).

Traditionally a prime brokerage business would be self-financing, as a hedge fund would hypothecate (place) a portfolio of securities as collateral, and then the prime broker would either pledge those assets under a tri-party pledge agreement or re-hypothecate (lend) that portfolio to another market counterparty in order to generate cash. For fixed income portfolios this is typically done under a repo arrangement rather than a lending arrangement as is the case for equities. Allowing the prime broker to re-hypothecate assets historically kept down the cost of borrowing money for hedge funds. It was unlimited re-hypothecation arrangements that led to a number of issues during the Lehman bankruptcy and consequently today limits are put in place to restrict the amount of the collateral portfolio that can be subsequently lent on. In the US there is a regulatory maximum re-hypothecation limit of 140% of indebtedness, and it is widely expected that other regulators may implement similar restrictions in the future.

## Securities Lending (Short Book)

In order to enter into a short position in a security a hedge fund will typically have to ensure that they have located stock to deliver prior to selling. On the day of settlement they will then need to borrow the stock in order to deliver this to the purchaser in the normal settlement process. The prime broker plays a pivotal role in this process by being the primary lender to the hedge fund of stock that they may wish to short.

It isn't sufficient simply to find the stock in the first place however, as once a hedge fund has identified a stock that they wish to short they clearly want to be able to maintain the short position until their investment thesis changes. The largest (non-investment) risk to a hedge fund of maintaining a short position is therefore that the stock is recalled by the prime broker. This risk can be evaluated by considering the inventory of assets that are available to the prime broker to lend and *this is a key differentiator* between different securities lending teams.

Securities financing teams can source their inventory from a number of different places ranging from large internal pools of assets, or from different external lenders that have their own large pools such as pension funds, asset managers, and sovereign wealth funds. Depending on the source(s) of the inventory and the type of collateral to be posted the borrow costs may vary meaningfully, and the stability of the borrows can also vary along with the ability to replace the short in a recall situation. When comparing the securities lending capability of a prime broker attention should be paid not only to general collateral stock, but also to the ability of the team to source hard to borrow stocks ("specials") where there is a greater probability of recall.

A further key role of a securities lending team is to provide market colour, indicative borrow rates, and the potential changes in stock loan availability to clients.


## Synthetic Prime Brokerage

As an alternative to obtaining financing through the traditional cash prime brokerage method described above hedge funds may utilise synthetic prime brokerage arrangements in which cash or securities are deposited with a prime broker as margin to cover equity positions obtained through swap. These swaps can be offered on an individual stock basis through a contract for difference ('CFD') or on a basket of stocks as a portfolio total return swap. In this manner the leverage provided is embedded within the derivative positions.

It is important in practice that a prime broker's traditional and synthetic prime brokerage offerings work seamlessly alongside one another. Prime brokers should be able to demonstrate a robust infrastructure covering execution, booking, and reporting with little manual intervention. Where these two offerings are provided in an integrated manner, the decision whether to use traditional or synthetic prime brokerage is still often a complex one and may vary by market. To further complicate matters, there are operationally different synthetic prime brokerage arrangements which result in slightly different set-ups and cash flows.

The advantages of a synthetic prime brokerage set-up are that it can:

- Allow a hedge fund to access certain markets that they can't access through physical securities e.g. some Asian markets where regulatory registrations may make set up economically or operationally unviable.

- Reduce the counterparty exposure of the hedge fund to the prime broker – In a synthetic prime brokerage set up a small (relative to the total portfolio size) amount of cash is deposited with the prime broker as margin. The total exposure to the prime broker is therefore limited to the amount of margin deposited plus any unrealised P&L from the swap portfolio. It is possible to reduce this second component by resetting the swap on a periodic basis (typically monthly) and sweeping any positive P&L away from the prime broker.

- Enable a hedge fund to gain the economic benefit of owning a share portfolio without some of the operational burdens such as maintaining records, monitoring corporate actions, undertaking regular reconciliations and managing re-hypothecation limits.

- Allow new structures to be used by hedge funds e.g. certain funds are not permitted to take leverage or short exposure in cash form.

The disadvantages of the synthetic prime brokerage set up are that it can:

- Remove the opportunity for corporate activism as the hedge fund does not retain beneficial ownership of the stock, so whilst the client will receive a dividend, there are no voting rights.

- Potentially only be applied to part of a portfolio. There are differences in how synthetic portfolios are viewed in different jurisdictions.

A hedge fund manager must understand the methodology the prime broker uses to determine the amount of margin required for a given swap portfolio, and care should also be taken to understand whether those margin terms may vary, particularly in stressed market conditions. It may be possible for larger funds, or for those that are willing to commit to various levels of financing for example to "lock up" their margin terms.

## PART 4 – DERIVATIVES PRIME BROKERAGE

### Listed Derivatives

Whether used as a risk-taking instrument or as a hedging tool, listed derivatives (futures and options) are widely used in hedge fund strategies, and therefore coverage of these instruments is a key requirement for prime brokers.

Listed futures and options are executed on an exchange by a designated execution broker, and then these trades are given up to a clearing broker (typically a well-capitalised bank which may be different to the execution broker) who faces the clearinghouse that becomes the central counterparty to the trade. The role of the clearing broker is to ensure the efficient settlement of the market, and in keeping books and records on the positions entered into by its clients. The clearer will monitor the risk in their client's portfolios, and be responsible for the collection of initial margin, and managing the P&L exchange of variation margin on the client's behalf vs. the clearinghouse.

A prime brokerage service for listed derivatives is a full trade cycle role that requires significant investment in technology to create an integrated execution and clearing platform that can handle significant volume. There are a significant number of futures markets and exchanges, and investment in direct execution and clearing memberships on as many exchanges as possible will allow a higher level of straight-through-processing (STP) and ultimately a reduced credit and operational risk when compared with the use of third party clearers. The experience of the firm in servicing listed derivative portfolios is critical here as there are significant variations across exchanges in the market rules, the handling of exercise and assignments, clearing cut-offs, and reporting requirements.

## OTC Clearing (& Intermediation)

Over-the-Counter (OTC) derivatives traditionally traded bilaterally under ISDA. They quickly gained popularity in the last 20 years as a flexible hedging tool for various types of risk across a range of markets. OTC derivatives.

The first prime brokerage development for OTC derivatives was intermediation, where the derivative trade is given up to a prime broker (similar to an FX PB arrangement), who enters the agreed trade as principal and has a trade with its client and an equal and opposite trade with the original executing bank.

Following the financial crisis, a strong program of regulatory reform has demanded that certain types of OTC derivatives, credit default swaps ('CDS') and interest rate swaps, be cleared on CCPs, (central counterparties, akin to derivative exchanges, such as LCH, CME, Eurex). In the US clearing was mandated in 2013 under Dodd-Frank for a number of vanilla OTC derivatives products. Similarly, in Europe the obligatory clearing of certain instruments is expected to phased-in from 2016, depending on the exact instrument and domicile of the counterparties. To add further complexity, depending on the region and CCP there are different sets of products that have to be cleared as well as that can be cleared, reflecting the local mandates and liquidity of the markets.

These reforms will mean that many hedge funds will be required to set-up an OTC clearing broker relationship, potentially with their existing prime broker. Clients will need to understand what will need to be cleared, versus what can continue to be held bilaterally or intermediated. There are, however, positive reasons for clearing as much of a portfolio as possible, not just what is necessary: improvement in counterparty risk and credit lines, better pricing, improved segregation of collateral, adoption of STP, margin and collateral efficiency, and the ability to cross-margin with listed derivatives. Regulations in multiple regions are similarly influencing electronic execution of OTC derivatives and clients should consider the ability to transact over a platform at the same time they are assessing building the infrastructure for clearing.

The choice of clearing broker(s) will be key for any client, involving the assessment of multiple items: credit quality, experience in the market, commitment to the service, derivatives expertise, pricing, ability to offer consulting, value-added services, bespoke operational assistance, etc. Clients should also bear in mind that, similar to intermediation, OTC clearing capacity is a limited resource and that clearing brokers will only extend services to those clients that they believe that can offer a long-lasting, diverse and, unsurprisingly, profitable relationship.

## FX Prime Brokerage

Foreign exchange ('FX') prime brokerage allows margin, liquidity and operational efficiencies through principal intermediation or 'give-up'. By consolidating trades through one central prime broker, clients enjoy the full portfolio benefit of offsetting trades while benefitting from one single confirmation and settlement partner. Furthermore, FX prime brokerage clients gain access to liquidity venues such as Electronic Communication Networks (ECNs) and have the ability to efficiently start trading relationships with a broad range of counterparties.

Part of the genesis of FX prime brokerage was the mitigation of credit risks and, conversely, broadening market access for clients. The choice of a well-capitalised prime broker can ensure that clients' money is better protected from a risk of default, and can give clients wider market access than they could achieve on their own to liquidity sources. This will also be achieved with a significantly lighter documentation burden than having several bilateral relationships as there is only a need for a single ISDA to be negotiated. A prime broker can also facilitate best access to the electronic liquidity platforms.

The prime broker's coverage in terms of products and currencies is a basic criterion. The FX market has a variety of different products that can be traded to take risks, including spot, forwards, Non-Deliverable forwards (NDFs) and options (either 'vanilla' or 'exotic'), and a range of currencies from highly liquid majors, to non-deliverable currencies that are settled in USD, or 'frontier' currencies from emerging markets. The manager should ensure that the prime broker has sufficient capabilities to clear and settle the FX products required for the fund's strategies.

In a similar manner to the service available for listed derivatives, a prime broker can assist a client that manages one or more funds or managed accounts in the splitting and allocation of trades and, potentially, 'reverse give-ups' to other prime brokers on associated funds or accounts.

## PART 5 – POST-TRADE SERVICING

### Operational Support

A prime brokerage arrangement maximises operational efficiencies as, at its core, a prime brokerage service is a post-trade operational support platform that facilitates its hedge fund clients transacting across different markets, instruments and asset classes. It helps a hedge fund manager to rationalise the day-to-day operational relationships that it maintains, and reduces the infrastructure burden and cost by simplifying operational flows and accordingly reduces operational risks. A vital role of any prime broker is as a keeper of books and records, and it is critical that these are handled accurately.

A key differentiator will be the standard of client service offered, encompassing technology, reporting, and relationship management. Trade flows should be STP with real-time reporting via FTP and web portals. 24 hour global or 'follow the sun' support from experienced staff who understand the client's business needs is a key part of a compelling prime brokerage offering.

The client services teams at a prime broker are the frontline of this operational support with relationship managers typically acting as a point of escalation and single point of contact who co-ordinates with the other product experts and service desks within the bank. Hedge funds should expect to have an almost daily interaction with the client service team, and those that require a higher level of day-to-day operational support should ensure that they understand the support on offer from their prime broker, and its coverage across different markets and time zones.

Prime brokerage relationships are ultimately partnerships, and regular reviews of the working practices between a hedge fund and a prime broker are essential in order to help the hedge fund improve their processes, and ensure high service levels are delivered by the prime broker. These reviews should incorporate all roles within both organisations including, but not limited to, the trading, operations, portfolio management, and business development teams at a hedge fund with the execution, client services, relationship management, prime brokerage sales, capital introduction, and consulting teams at the prime broker. It is important that these reviews are done in the context of the balances and revenues that a hedge fund may have with their prime broker.

**Clearing, Settlement and Custody**

Clearing (managing the actions between trade date and settlement date) and settling (the exchange of cash and securities between buyer and seller) trades for its hedge fund clients across a range of markets and asset classes is one of the primary operational roles of a prime broker. Furthermore the prime broker is also likely to act as a custodian whereby it is responsible for the safekeeping of those purchased securities in addition to non-cash collateral. When selecting a prime broker a hedge fund should be very clear about which markets and instruments they wish to access and ensure that the prime broker is able to process and hold in custody those positions, and that the margin terms are acceptable.

As a bank is unlikely to have a clearing presence in every market, prime brokers will often have sub-custodial relationships with local clearing institutions. In order to understand their potential counterparty risks, hedge fund managers should understand which parts of their portfolio may be held with non-affiliated entities, which those entities are, and the manner in which those assets are held.

In recent times there have been various initiatives in Europe relating to fund structures; a number of which have had a deep impact on post-trade processes, especially the latest iteration of UCITS and the Alternative Investment Fund Managers Directive (AIFMD). AIFMD follows the UCITS Directive in requiring managers of alternative investment funds (AIFs) to appoint a depositary.

The entity that performs this depositary function is expected to act independently and safeguard the interests of the fund investors. The depositary has an oversight function, which it can't delegate, that includes monitoring the fund's cash flow and ensuring transactions are carried out in accordance with both AIFMD and the fund's constitutional documents. In addition they are responsible for the safekeeping of the fund assets, but may appoint a separate custodian to do this, such as a prime broker, if required. There has been a major impact on custodian banks as a result of these initiatives. For example, AIFMD introduces a strict liability upon depositaries and custodian banks for the return of any client asset without undue delay should the asset be lost.

Hedge Funds generate asset-related P&Ls and fees and expenses in a variety of currencies. The management of currency exposures is conducted through the prime broker.

**Asset Servicing**

The prime broker in its role as a custodian will often provide a variety of asset servicing functions for the securities held in custody for the hedge fund. This will include the processing of both voluntary and mandatory corporate actions (rights issues, takeovers etc.), participation in the voting process for AGM motions, and the reconciliation and receipt of dividends and interest payments. Whilst these operational functions are not the most high profile elements of a prime brokerage service, this role is particularly important for event driven/activist strategies and those that are particularly sensitive to corporate events.

**Regulatory Reporting**

In its role as a central counterparty to a hedge fund, a prime broker is in a position to aggregate a significant amount of data that the manager needs to meet its various regulatory reporting requirements. The form of this reporting can be, for example, systemic risk reporting under AIFMD, or the provision of trade information to central repositories under EMIR or Dodd Frank.

A hedge fund manager should understand the scope of what reporting the prime broker is able to provide, and what experience they have as the reporting requirements in different jurisdictions may vary significantly. In the US under Dodd Frank, reporting is only required for OTC derivatives, whilst in Europe EMIR includes listed derivatives, and the collateral associated with the trade as well.

PART 6 – OTHER SERVICES

The prime brokerage business is fairly mature and the banks that provide these services have looked to offer other services in order to differentiate themselves in a highly competitive marketplace. There are a number of ways that they may seek to do so including enhanced execution services, helping clients to reduce their margin and manage their collateral, and developing their businesses through capital introductions and consulting services.

## Execution

It is essential to consider the prime broker's execution franchise when evaluating a potential relationship as due to various operational economies a prime broker is typically one of the primary execution counterparties for a hedge fund. The breadth of market access that can be offered by the prime broker and the extent that this is integrated with the rest of the prime brokerage technology platform is critical. The larger the number of the direct execution memberships held by a prime broker the higher the level of STP and therefore greater potential operational efficiencies.

Across different fund strategies, and throughout a fund's lifecycle and there may be a significant variation in the amount of execution support a hedge fund requires. When considering such platforms, managers should understand the transaction types the prime broker can cover, the speed and latency that can be offered, connectivity to exchanges and the order types supported. An execution partner should enable clients to execute in whichever manner they feel the most comfortable with, from high touch to very low touch.

The highest-touch execution service is typically provided by a sales or sales-trader within the bank. This person will provide trade ideas, market colour, and flow analysis in addition to suggesting appropriate execution strategies and actively sourcing liquidity. These coverage desks are generally organised by product type, and for clients that wish to execute in a wide range of markets across asset classes they may need to deal with multiple teams within the bank. For clients that don't wish to do this, 'care' desks act as an outsourced execution team across all asset classes whereby orders can be given to the desk to be executed at market, or to be worked within certain defined parameters.

The quantitative side of execution has developed significantly in recent years, and many banks have created automated solutions for their clients in order to achieve consistent execution results from day to day. These solutions are based on a pre-defined algorithm ('Algo') and may have industry standard benchmarks such as VWAP (volume weighted average price) or TWAP (time weighted average price), or be value-added and seek to reduce the cost of slippage for the client. In addition to accessing algos that have already been created, some banks will offer bespoke solutions tailored to a specific hedge fund's requirements.

The lowest touch form of executing from a prime broker's standpoint is also the one that requires a significant technology investment on the hedge fund's side. In this way, the hedge fund leverages a prime broker's existing direct market access (DMA) pipes in order to place buy and sell orders directly on an exchange. The most common form of DMA is when a piece of execution software (a 'screen') created by the execution bank or a third party is installed at the hedge fund who can then control and monitor their own orders. A more sophisticated version of this set-up is possible whereby the hedge fund itself creates their own execution software and algorithms connected to their trading system which then allows full 'no-touch' trading. A good prime broker will have dedicated teams of specialists to assist in the initial set-up and testing, as well as for providing ongoing advice and assistance and the day-to-day monitoring of orders.

The prime broker may also be able to provide execution advisory services in order to assist clients with improving their execution quality as well as analysis services of the various executing brokers which the hedge fund manager uses.

## Portfolio Margining & Cross Margining

Obtaining an understanding of a prime broker's margining methodologies is important for clients who want to achieve the greatest capital efficiency.

Traditionally the amount of margin required from a hedge fund would be determined using linear margins applied to individual positions based on static grids. Prime brokers may now have more sophisticated methods for calculating margin, and where it is available, cross-margining may significantly reduce the amount of margin or collateral that is required to be deposited with the prime broker. These risk-based margin systems attempt to set margin requirements based on the overall risk of the portfolio (rather than simply adding all the positions together) and typically provide significant benefit to conservative and more diversified or market-neutral portfolios.

There may be a significant variation in a prime broker's ability to provide capital efficiency to a diversified portfolio. Some prime brokers may only provide US Portfolio Margining for an equities portfolio, whilst others may go significantly further and be able to offer cross-margining across a range of instruments and asset classes.

A maximum amount of margin efficiency will be obtained by having a single prime broker who has a view across the entire portfolio which should allow for the maximum number of offsets. The credit exposure to that single counterparty has been reduced through the cross-margining, however some hedge funds may prefer to have multiple counterparties even if it means they are not as capital efficient as possible.


## Client Collateral Management/Transformation

Collateral Optimisation is the process by which a prime broker helps their hedge fund clients ensure that they are using the assets they own (both cash and securities) in the most efficient way possible to collateralise their exposures.

Collateral optimisation isn't a new concept but the regulatory and market environment for posted collateral has shifted dramatically in recent years. New regulations that increase the need for collateralisation of bilateral trades, or the central clearing requirements of EMIR and Dodd Frank, have made this an increasingly important focus for hedge funds. In addition, there may be an imperative due to a forecast shift from cash to non-cash collateral, a sharp rise in the number of collateral movements and regulatory reporting, and the increasingly complex network of counterparties, CCPs and clearing brokers.

Clients may hold lower quality assets that are ineligible for collateral purposes and some prime brokers offer solutions to transform (upgrade) those assets into eligible collateral, allowing for the efficient allocation of collateral. This is an increasingly important additional service for a prime broker to offer to its hedge fund clients.

**Capital Introduction**

Capital introduction fulfils a dual role, acting as an agent of hedge fund investors whilst providing a range of value added services to the prime broker's hedge fund clients.

For investors, a capital introductions team act as a no-cost information resource for all matters related to portfolio construction and manager selection. A capital introductions team identifies institutional allocators globally and develops longstanding relationships based on an understanding of their specific portfolio requirements. Investor groups that they typically engage with include family offices, wealth managers, fund of hedge funds, pension, consultants and sovereign wealth funds. Through dialogue and at the investors' initiative, the Capital Introductions team can make targeted introductions to external investment managers. Capital introduction teams typically have a global presence and possess expertise in specific hedge fund strategies, investor geographies and segments. Organisation and participation in dedicated events and conferences is often a preferred means of introducing interested investors to relevant managers.

For hedge funds, a capital introduction team provides strategic guidance on profile raising and business development across a fund's lifecycle, from launch, to growth and then maturity. Capital introduction teams identify appetite across different investor segments globally and then map out routes of access to these groups. Often capital introduction teams can also assist with roadshow planning and profile-raising campaigns. It is important to note that Capital Introductions does not replicate or replace a hedge fund's marketing function but is a resource that can be utilised to boost it. In an environment of increasing regulatory oversight, capital introduction can also provide best practice guidance on hedge fund interactions with prospective investors, but it does not intend to replace a hedge fund's compliance or legal counsel.


## Consulting

Hedge fund consulting services draw upon the breadth and depth of the prime broker's industry knowledge to act as an outsourced human resource and business management function, facilitating thoughtful construction and growth. Consultants aim to closely support decision making around some of the most critical aspects of business building, including identifying investment and operational talent, the selection of service providers, and financial planning for business growth.

Consulting services teams can be structured as a group of fully-dedicated consultants or else may collectively draw on the varied and individual abilities across the prime brokerage teams at large. Each prime broker will have particular strong suits across areas of need, and an assessment should be conducted to determine best fit. Consulting services can be valuable at all stages of a hedge fund's lifecycle, but some teams will have more experience assisting early stage managers, while others will be more experienced dealing with the particular issues impacting more mature managers.

At the start-up phase of fund construction, hedge fund consulting teams can provide a manager with important tools to help increases the chances for business success. Experienced consulting teams will also be able to identify an appropriate list of service providers such as administrators, auditors, outsourced legal and compliance, and board directors that specialise in catering to the particular needs of early stage managers. Hedge fund consulting groups may provide assistance in other areas such as locating real estate, selecting technological solutions, and even provide guidance on the structuring of deal terms for strategic partnerships.

"As Consulting Services can be a gateway to all the necessary service providers used by a new hedge fund management company, the appointment of the prime broker is usually considered the key appointment for start-ups"

Managers with longer histories should also be able to benefit from prime broker hedge fund consultation. As funds consider the launch of additional investment programs, consulting services can provide competitive analyses and help guide positioning of products in the marketplace. Transitional planning, the potential sale or repurchase of general partnership interests, and the distribution of equity ownership are all areas whereby consultants should be able to lend some industry perspective.

As Consulting Services can be a gateway to all the necessary service providers used by a new hedge fund management company, the appointment of the prime broker is usually considered the key appointment for start-ups.

147

## PART 7 – DOCUMENTATION

Depending on the type and number of instruments that a hedge fund intends to trade the legal documentation can vary from relatively simple to fairly complex. Examples of the sorts of documentation that may be required are:

- Prime Brokerage Agreement

The Prime Brokerage Agreement details the scope of the relationship between the hedge fund and its prime broker and the obligations of each party. This covers topics such as custody, collateral, the handling of client money, commission and margin terms, re-hypothecation limits etc.

- Global Master Securities Lending Agreement ("GMSLA")

A standardised agreement that details the terms of securities lending transactions for equities and bonds.

- Global Master Repurchase Agreement ("GMRA")

A standardised document that details the terms of repurchase (repo) transactions.

- ISDA Master Agreement

A standardised agreement that sets out the terms that will apply to all OTC derivative transactions between the hedge fund and the prime broker. The terms of a Master Agreement can be tailored through the use of a schedule which will detail any additions or amendments to the Master. A Credit Support Annex (CSA) is added if there is to be a transfer of collateral between the two parties, and defines the terms under which that collateral is posted.

- Master Confirmation Agreement ("MCA")

A Master Confirmation Agreement is used to simplify the documentation for transactions entered into under an ISDA. The MCA makes the confirmation process more efficient by reducing the content of the confirmations to material economic terms rather than exchanging a full confirmation as detailed in the ISDA Master Agreement.

- FOA Clearing Agreement

An agreement that details the terms that will apply for all exchange traded derivatives transactions.

- FOA Clearing Module

The FOA Clearing Module was created post EMIR to enables firms to clear listed and OTC derivatives by using their FOA Clearing Agreement without needing to sign terms with each CCP.

- FX Prime Brokerage Agent Agreement

This agreement allows a prime brokerage client to trade using their prime broker's credit lines and profile, and reduces the need for document negotiation with each of their executing brokers.

- Custody Agreement

An agreement that details the terms under which the prime broker will custody assets for the hedge fund.

- Give Up Agreement

An agreement that details the terms under which the prime broker will accept listed derivative transactions from a third party execution broker.

- Designation Notice

An agreement that details the terms under which the prime broker will accept listed foreign exchange and OTC derivative transactions from a third party execution broker.

This is by no means a comprehensive list as UCITS funds for example will also have pledge and account control agreements, and there may be additional documentation required to determine the relevant tax location such as Cross-border swaps representation letter (US person election) etc.

Although the agreements cited above are based on standardised documents the terms will vary and new hedge fund managers may need to negotiate some of the terms, fees and conditions.

## PART 8 – SELECTING A PRIME BROKER, INCLUDING SUGGESTED KEY QUESTIONS

Societe Generale Prime Services is a separate business line within the Capital Markets Division of Societe Generale. As the bank's Prime Brokerage business, it is truly cross-asset, offering a unique combination of execution, clearing, custody and financing services from a single business line; with a multi-asset and multi-instrument brokerage platform across Listed Derivatives, Equities (Cash/synthetic), FX, Fixed Income and OTC Cleared. As the largest execution and clearing broker of ETD's with a 11% market share, it provides clients with unrivalled access to 125+ markets and exchange venues, an extensive pool of liquidity and tailored value added services – it is well positioned to service the needs of Hedge Funds, Institutions and Proprietary Trading Groups globally.

The full service platform offers access to significant securities financing capabilities, an award winning capital introduction's business and best-in-class cross-margin capabilities as well as straight-through-processing with an industry leading post-trade platform aligned with Societe Generale's extensive research product.

The quality of its Prime Brokerage offering has been recognised by the industry having been awarded Best European Prime Broker by Hedge

Week and Hedge Fund Journal and Best Global Multi-Asset Prime Brokerage in 2015 by CTA Intelligence and Capital Introduction' awards in the US. Societe Generale Prime Services is in the top 3 of brokers according to CFTC rankings of assets under management. Furthermore, Preqin, the alternative assets industry's leading source of data and intelligence, ranked Societe Generale Prime Services as number one in terms of CTA market share.

## CONTACT INFORMATION

Societe Generale International Limited

**Primary Contact:** James Skeggs,

Global Head of Alternative Investment Consulting

+44 (0)20 7676 8225

James.Skeggs@newedge.com

Switchboard: +44 (0)20 7676 8300

**Website:** www.sgcib.com/primeservices

**Address:** 10 Bishops Square, London, E1 6EG

# Chapter 8. Legal Services For European Hedge Funds

By Gus Black and Craig Borthwick of Dechert LLP

## About the authors

**Gus Black** *focuses his practice on investment funds (emphasizing private equity, debt and hedge funds), establishing and restructuring international asset management businesses, corporate and commercial transactions in the asset management sector and general UK financial services regulation.*

*In the sphere of private fund formation, he has advised sponsors and cornerstone investors on the structuring, re-structuring, formation and investment of numerous funds and other co-investment structures ranging widely in size, strategy and focus (including numerous hedge strategies, hybrid, private equity, public and private debt, emerging markets, clean tech/energy, agriculture, infrastructure, commodities and real estate). He has advised on funds established in various jurisdictions including Jersey, Guernsey, Cayman Islands, BVI, Luxembourg, Ireland, Singapore, Mauritius, Delaware and England. He also advises on a range of portfolio investments, secondaries and other portfolio transactions.*

*Gus Black is also recommended as a leading lawyer in his field in Chambers UK 2015 which states that he is recognised for his broad practice and capability on multi-jurisdictional mandates and provides client testimony that he is "incredibly knowledgeable - when we're looking to launch quite a bespoke product he has almost always had experience in something similar."*

*His publications include the "Private Equity Funds" chapter of Sweet & Maxwell's Law and Regulation of Investment Management and the UK. chapter of the European Lawyer Reference Series on Hedge Funds.*

*Craig Borthwick advises on the formation and structuring of a variety of investment funds and fund platforms as well as providing ongoing advice on general corporate, compliance and regulatory issues. He also advises on service provider documentation. His practice is focused on alternative asset management. Start-ups and seeding deals form a significant part of his practice.*

*Prior to joining Dechert in 2012, Craig Borthwick spent time on secondment to a global hedge fund manager.*

*He was part of the AIMA working committee on AIFMD, in particular relating to delegation arrangements.*

## About Dechert LLP

Dechert is a global specialist law firm with offices in 28 cities around the world. The partnership is focused on sectors with the greatest complexities, legal intricacies and highest regulatory demands, the firm excels at delivering practical commercial judgment and deep legal expertise for high-stakes matters. In an increasingly challenging environment, clients look to Dechert to serve them in ways that are faster, sharper and leaner without compromising excellence. The firm is relentless in serving its clients – delivering the best of the partnership to them with entrepreneurial energy and seamless collaboration in a way that is distinctively Dechert.

Dechert is part of the "Global 20," which recognizes law firms with the largest global presence and involvement in the biggest, most complex and most diverse cross-border matters over the past year (Law360, 2016). The firm thinks globally, and has expertise that crosses borders. The lawyers of Dechert speak more than 40 languages. There are 32 standout practices recognized by Chambers Global, 2016. Among the top 20 global law firms, Dechert is rated #1 for service delivery in The Legal 500 Client Intelligence Report, 2015.

# PART 1 – INTRODUCTION

Dechert LLP is consistently ranked as one of the leading firms in the world for hedge fund formation by the major legal directories. Whilst the firm represents many of the world's largest hedge funds, it also has a very strong tradition of business start-up work for new managers and has launched hundreds of new hedge funds in London, New York and other markets.

# PART 2 – ESTABLISHMENT OF A HEDGE FUND

## 1. OVERVIEW

Hedge fund structuring is often perceived as a well-trodden path and largely a simple exercise of replication. Any such illusion of simplicity is either the work of a good lawyer or the advice of a bad one. Whilst there is certainly a degree of consistency in the structuring of many hedge fund products, there are a range of considerations a prudent hedge fund manager should take into account in determining the most

155

appropriate structure for his first or his next product and a range of different possible outcomes.

The 'well-trodden path' has also become increasingly complicated by a range of recent market developments, including the institutionalisation of hedge fund management (and the connected convergence of traditional 'long only' asset management with absolute return), the blurring of liquid and illiquid strategies, particularly in the credit/debt space, the more onerous regulatory framework in which hedge fund managers now have to operate and various perceptional issues around hedge funds and their role in modern day finance.

> "The 'well-trodden path' has also become increasingly complicated by a range of recent developments, including the institutionalisation of hedge fund management, and the connected convergence of traditional 'long-only' asset management with absolute return."

This chapter seeks to provide a high level overview of some of the key issues a new or existing hedge fund manager should consider in structuring a new hedge fund.

## 2. INVESTORS; THE STARTING POINT

### 2.1 Initial and Target Investor Base

The fund's initial and target investor base should be the starting point. Ideally, a fund structure should be established which meets the needs of both. If this is not possible, a balance will need to be struck between meeting the needs of the fund's initial investors (who will likely be critical in terms of the fund reaching a viable size) and the fund's longer term target investors.

## 2.2  Investor Jurisdiction and Tax Preferences

Investors will seek to invest in a fund vehicle that ensures no or minimal tax leakage at the fund level and does not place them at an undue disadvantage in terms of their own taxation.

From the perspective of investors in the U.S. and certain other jurisdictions, the character of the fund from a tax perspective is highly relevant here.  The fund may be regarded as an opaque entity (e.g. a corporate) or as a transparent entity (e.g. a partnership or an entity treated as a partnership for U.S. tax purposes[1] ).  It is possible to satisfy the tax requirements of each type of investor in a single fund structure by using a "master-feeder" fund structure (see section 3.2 below).

## 2.3  Other Investor Type Considerations

The hedge fund industry investor base has changed significantly over the years, as institutional investors have increasingly sought more exposure to 'absolute return' strategies. The needs and wants of institutional investors can vary considerably, depending on what type of entity they are, which funding sources they are using and which tax, legal and regulatory regimes they are subject to.   Familiarity with and the ability to deal easily with different types of investor on a global basis – pension funds, private banks, fund of funds, insurance companies, foundations, family offices and any number of other myriad possibilities – is one of the things a new hedge fund manager should consider when selecting service providers.

## 2.4  Accessing Capital; Target Investors and Marketing Considerations

The Cayman Islands remains a popular jurisdiction for hedge fund managers seeking to raise capital on a global basis. US investors, who remain the largest source of capital for hedge funds, are familiar with

---

[1] It is possible for certain non-partnership entities to be treated as tax transparent for US tax purposes by the entity making a Form 8832 election (known as a 'check-the-box' election).

Cayman Islands domiciled fund structures, as are institutional investors in many other jurisdictions.

Recent regulatory change in Europe – most particularly the Alternative Investment Fund Managers Directive ("AIFMD") – has made the marketing of non-European domiciled funds in Europe more difficult (albeit the UK and Switzerland, two key sources of hedge fund capital, remain generally accessible). In addition, we have seen a trend away from allocations to the Cayman Islands on the part of certain types of European investor. A manager wishing to raise a significant amount of capital from within Europe (particularly continental Europe) should carefully consider how appropriate a Cayman-only structure will be (see section 4 below).

3. *STRUCTURE; KEY CONSIDERATIONS*

3.1 **Open-Ended or Closed-Ended; Liquidity**

Funds can be open-ended or closed-ended. Open-ended funds allow investors to subscribe for and redeem their investment in the fund on a regular basis. Closed-ended funds generally limit investment to one or more initial subscription dates and thereafter investors are generally unable to redeem their interests at will (with returns of capital being made at set intervals or at the end of the life of the fund).

A hedge fund will be typically be open-ended due to most hedge fund strategies being relatively liquid in nature (and because hedge fund investors will expect similar liquidity in their investment terms). Closed-ended structures are more typically used for private equity strategies or other specialist and less liquid strategies, including real estate, infrastructure investment or debt (including direct lending funds).

In recent years, there has been some convergence between liquid and illiquid strategies, in particular in the credit space. There have been different approaches to these hybrid structures. Some funds combine traditional elements of 'hedge' and 'private equity' structures. When setting up an open-ended fund to manage illiquid assets, managers will need to carefully manage liquidity and consider carefully how they will meet redemption requests in a range of different scenarios.

## 3.2    Standalone or Master-Feeder Structure

As discussed under "Investor Jurisdiction and Tax Preferences" above, the types of investors the fund wishes to target will determine whether the fund is structured as a standalone fund or as a master-feeder fund.

Example: Master feeder fund structure

US taxpayers will generally require a tax transparent fund vehicle through which to invest whilst non-US investors and US tax-exempt investors will require a tax opaque fund vehicle. Both types of tax treatment can be accommodated in a master-feeder fund structure. The master-feeder structure will be comprised of a tax-transparent master fund with one or more feeder funds. Non-US investors and US tax-exempts will invest through a tax opaque feeder and US taxpayers will invest through a tax transparent feeder (or alternatively in the tax transparent master fund directly).   Other feeders can be structured for other reasons or other types of investor, as required.

Whilst the different needs of investors for tax opaque and tax transparent vehicles could be achieved by running parallel funds, a master-feeder fund structure enhances the critical mass of investable assets (which will be managed at the level of the master fund), and avoids the need for the investment manager to split trades or engage in re-balancing trades between the parallel structures and for the fund to enter into duplicate arrangements with service providers and counterparties. Additionally, it creates greater economies of scale for the day-to-day management and administration of the fund, which generally leads to lower operational and transaction costs.

If only a tax opaque or tax transparent vehicle is required in light of the intended initial and longer term investor base, then a standalone vehicle with the appropriate tax characteristics should be sufficient and simpler.

### 3.3 Single Cell or Umbrella Structure; Single vs. Multiple Strategies

If the fund will have one investment strategy and one portfolio of assets, a single portfolio vehicle will likely be appropriate. If the fund is to run multiple portfolios of assets, an umbrella structure may be more appropriate. The umbrella structure allows an investment manager to run multiple strategies through one fund structure (with one set of service providers) without the need to establish separate fund structures for each strategy. Umbrella structures can reduce costs and documentation. However, in some situations, it will be more efficient (and attractive to investors) to run the different strategies through different fund vehicles, rather than an umbrella structure.

A number of jurisdictions have introduced structures which, as a matter of local law, offer segregation between different portfolios (or sub funds). Not all of these structures have been tested in the courts of other jurisdictions, including in the US. Where this is the case, there is a residual risk that such structure will not be enforceable.

Another factor to consider is investor perception. Regardless of actual risk, investors might be cautious as to the risk of contagion between different portfolios or sub-funds where a portfolio or sub-fund suffers a loss and the ability for counterparties to claim against the umbrella structure as a whole.

## 3.4    Third-Party Fund Platforms

The increase in hedge fund regulation and the associated costs of establishing a hedge fund management business have increased barriers to entry. This has encouraged a growing number of would be start-up managers to use a third-party fund platform as an alternative to establishing their own fund structure.

Third-party fund platforms are generally umbrella structures that allow promoters to "plug and play" by joining the platform with their own separately managed sub-funds or portfolios of assets. Platforms may benefit from shared costs and potential distribution through capital introduction capabilities. Some third-party platforms provide regulatory cover as well as a fund structure, which means that the manager does not need to obtain its own FCA authorisation.

The downsides of launching on a platform include cost (with costs calculated on an AUM basis, platforms can be more expensive for larger funds), a lack of control (an investment manager is a service provider and so is unlikely to have any representation on the platform's board), the investment manager may have limited (or no) choice in terms of service providers, and problems may arise if the investment manager wishes to move to its own platform or the platform itself goes out of business (for example, where moving the fund to another vehicle, there is a risk that an investment gain will be crystallised for tax purposes). In summary, platforms can be a simpler and cheaper way of getting started and building track record but, over the long term, the economics and lack of control is not viable or acceptable for most managers.

## 3.5  Managed Accounts

Whilst many investors are happy to invest in a fund vehicle offered to multiple investors, certain investors may seek or require greater control and transparency in relation to the management of their assets and have particular commercial requirements (e.g. as to strategy and leverage) which means it is either not possible or desirable for them to invest in a manager's main fund vehicle.

Traditionally, large long-only asset managers offered such investors managed accounts in respect of which the investor appointed its own custodian and appointed the manager to provide investment management and other services in relation to the management of the portfolio. This structure is less often used in the context of hedge fund strategies. The main reason for this is that hedge fund strategies typically use one or more prime brokers and multiple derivative counterparties. Most institutional clients will not wish to take on the administrative burden of establishing a structure from which such a portfolio can be operated and managed. To the extent these managers require a bespoke or private fund vehicle, such investors typically look to the hedge fund manager and/or a third party platform provider to provide a standalone fund in which the institutional investor is the sole participant (a 'fund of one').

## 4.  *JURISDICTION; WHERE SHOULD THE FUND BE DOMICILED?*

## 4.1  Overview

There is considerable competition between leading jurisdictions. Popular jurisdictions include, amongst others, the Cayman Islands, Ireland, Luxembourg and the U.S. (commonly Delaware when targeting U.S. investors); Malta, Bermuda, the British Virgin Islands, Mauritius, Jersey, Guernsey and Singapore.  In choosing a fund domicile, issues for consideration include the following:

162

(a)     the tax efficiency of establishing the fund in a jurisdiction, including how it will be regarded by tax authorities in investor jurisdictions;

(b)     the familiarity of the jurisdiction to the target investor base (a perceptional issue);

(c)     whether the jurisdiction will enhance or restrict the fund's ability to be marketed into certain jurisdictions or to certain target investor types;

(d)     whether laws and regulatory requirements governing the fund and service providers, investment and borrowing powers and restrictions, custody arrangements, confidentiality laws, banking secrecy laws, foreign exchange limitations etc. might make one jurisdiction more desirable in a particular case than another;

(e)     the nature and extent of anti-money laundering measures in any particular jurisdiction, which will go to its reputation and credibility[2] ;

(f)     whether the manager has pre-existing relationships in the jurisdiction – for example with service providers or directors;

(g)     whether the manager intends to build any management company substance in or near that jurisdiction and would therefore benefit for co-locating the manager and fund;

(h)     other proximity and time zone issues, depending on the manager personnel location and strategy;

(i)     whether there are sufficient local accountancy firms and law firms (and, if a fund is to be administered or have its assets custodied

---

[2] All member states of the EU (for example, Ireland, Luxembourg and the UK) are required to enact legislation and financial sector procedures in accordance with the European money laundering directive. In addition, all EU member states belong to the Financial Action Task Force ("FATF") and are thereby committed to implementing the FATF recommendations. In addition, the Isle of Man, Jersey, Guernsey, the Cayman Islands and other jurisdictions can also be regarded as having (or introducing) equivalent legislation.

locally, banks, local directors, custodians and administrators) to support the operation of the fund;

(j)     establishment costs, expenses and ongoing maintenance of the fund;

(k)     time to market, i.e., how long it will take to establish the fund; and

(l)     whether the jurisdiction chosen is politically stable and the attitude and familiarity of authorities in the jurisdiction towards hedge funds.


## 4.2     Key Fund Jurisdictions

### Cayman Islands

The Cayman Islands remains the jurisdiction of choice for most US and UK-based managers. The Cayman Islands is very familiar to institutional and international investors and offers flexible yet well developed accounting, legal and tax structures for funds backed up by high quality legal and accounting service providers and a recognised legal system for resolving disputes. There are no restrictions on the strategies that may be implemented through a Cayman fund and no limits on the types of investors that may invest in such a fund (provided that the fund may not be marketed to the public in the Cayman Islands).

A Cayman hedge fund can be established as a body corporate, limited partnership, unit trust or segregated portfolio company. Master-feeder fund structures can be established utilising all of these entities/structures with and without a Delaware feeder (see below). These structures all benefit from tax exemptions. The segregated portfolio company is an umbrella type structure.

The Cayman Islands offers an unrivalled collection of local and experienced hedge fund directors, as well as high-quality local service providers. It also permits Cayman funds to use administrators, custodians and other service providers based outside the Cayman Islands. Thus many Cayman structures are serviced by administrators and custodians based in jurisdictions such as Ireland and the US and prime brokers based in the UK and the US. In addition, the Cayman Islands has been efficient at ensuring that it keeps up with important developments in the US and Europe affecting alternative investment funds including regulatory requirements arising out of FATCA in the US and the AIFMD in the EEA. The Cayman Islands has also taken steps to ensure compliance with the OECD's common reporting standard.

The Cayman Islands also remains a relatively quick (and generally very cost-effective) jurisdiction in which to establish a hedge fund.

### Delaware

The hedge fund industry has its roots in Delaware and US taxable investors requiring a tax transparent vehicle in which to invest will typically prefer to invest in a Delaware feeder (normally in the form of a limited partnership or LLC).

### EEA Established Funds

Funds established outside the EEA may currently only be marketed into EEA countries in accordance with each jurisdiction's private placement regime. Certain EEA jurisdictions do not permit private placement or impose requirements that make it costly or complex to undertake marketing on a private placement basis. In contrast, funds established in the EEA may be marketed into other EEA jurisdictions utilising a passport introduced by AIFMD. Broadly speaking, this allows the fund to be marketed throughout the EEA by reference to a single set of rules with limited gold-plating on a jurisdiction-by-jurisdiction basis.

Ireland and Luxembourg are the most popular EEA jurisdictions for those primarily seeking investment from European investors. Both jurisdictions offer a range of fund products, including corporate, partnership, contractual, and in the case of Ireland, unit trust structures. Both jurisdictions also offer master-feeder structures and umbrella / segregated portfolio options.

Funds domiciled in Ireland and Luxembourg are required to use local administrators and depositary service providers. Ireland also requires that at least two of the fund's directors be Irish resident. While Luxembourg has no such requirement, it would usually be advisable to have at least one or two local directors.

## 5.    FUND DIRECTORS AND SERVICE PROVIDERS

### 5.1    **Fund Directors**

Companies (including general partners of partnerships) are required to appoint directors. Such directors will be subject to a number of statutory and fiduciary duties and will be required to approve certain actions taken by the company, including the appointment of service providers to the fund. However, hedge fund directors do not typically make investment decisions, responsibility for which is usually delegated to an investment manager. Likewise, day-to-day administration of the fund is delegated to the fund's administrator and custody is delegated to an appointed prime broker or custodian. The directors are required to maintain oversight of delegated activities.

Whilst it is common for a representative of the investment manager to sit on the board of directors, a company should look to appoint a majority of independent directors. This is usually fundamental to the tax structuring of a UK managed hedge fund, and is also important for a range of other reasons.

### 5.2    **Key Service Providers**

A hedge fund's key service providers are broadly as follows:

*Investment manager.* An investment management agreement will be entered into between the fund and the manager pursuant to which the manager is appointed on arm's length terms to provide portfolio management, risk management and marketing services.

*Prime brokers, depositary and trading counterparties.* The fund's prime brokers will custody, clear and settle trades entered into by the fund as well as providing access to financing and securities lending. Hedge funds will often appoint more than one prime broker as well as a number of other trading counterparties allowing them to access liquidity more effectively and also trade in a wide range of securities and through a wide range of derivative instruments.

Prime brokers extend capital so as to enable funds to acquire securities on a leveraged basis. Assets of the fund are used as collateral against the loan and the prime broker will have the right to rehypothecate the assets, usually up to a certain percentage of the amount borrowed. Prime brokers can extend the capital in a number of ways. This may include the simple extension of credit to allow a fund to acquire an asset as well as the provision of credit through the leverage inherent in derivative instruments.

Prime brokers may also undertake the role of clearing, settling and safe-keeping of the fund's assets. The ability for a prime broker to custody a fund's assets will depend on the country specific rules and regulations for the holding of assets and the scope of a prime brokers market coverage, including from a geographical perspective. Prime brokers may operate a sub-custodial network to provide coverage in the jurisdictions in which it does not have custody capabilities. One of the most important factors to consider is the manner in which assets are held in custody, in particular as to whether assets are segregated from those of other clients.

Prime brokers will often provide a capital introduction service which can be useful in helping a hedge fund manager raise capital in the fund's early years. Capital introduction may be wider than just introducing investors to hedge funds and includes providing strategic assistance to a fund manager seeking to market the fund as well as feedback on current market trends, investor sentiment, fund terms and other matters.

*Administrator.* The fund's administrator will typically be appointed to provide the following services: (i) registrar and transfer agent, responsible for the issue, redemption and transfer of fund shares or interests and ensuring that all subscription and redemption forms have been completed in full and in compliance with applicable anti-money laundering requirements; (ii) calculation of the fund's net asset value and management fees and performance fees (utilising series or equalisation accounting as applicable); (iii) general communication with investors, including the circulation of updated fund documentation and notices to investors (including ahead of shareholder meetings); and (iv) preparation of the fund's financial statements and providing assistance with the fund's audit.

## 6.    *UCITS*

An alternative (or a compliment) to the traditional hedge fund model?

UCITS are the most common form of investment fund in Europe. Traditionally, UCITS were used as investment vehicles by managers pursuing long-only and relative return strategies (and that overwhelmingly remains the case today). However, as interest in absolute return strategies has increased, asset managers pursuing 'traditional' investment strategies have increasingly developed their own absolute return type strategies.  Hedge fund managers have also increasingly utilised UCITS to access greater distribution potential with different investors. This has led to a convergence between traditional long-only asset management and absolute return asset management.

The attraction of UCITS as a way of structuring absolute return strategies derives from its marketability. The increased marketability of UCITS is largely a result of its liquidity and regulated status which gives many investors a certain level of comfort (and a perception that UCITS offers a safer product in which to invest).

UCITS benefit from a marketing passport which makes it relatively simple to market the product across Europe (and a number of other jurisdictions outside of Europe have made it relatively simple to register UCITS for public distribution).

Many European investors may be limited in their ability to invest in offshore hedge fund products as a matter of local law or regulation or, alternatively, as a result of internal allocation requirements. Many institutional investors are also limited as to the level of allocation they can make to alternative strategies - and UCITSare often deemed not to be 'alternatives' whether or not they pursue an absolute return strategy. As such, UCITS have a wider investor potential in Europe than traditional hedge fund products.

As a result of the foregoing, many hedge fund managers run absolute return strategies alongside their traditional hedge fund strategies. However, there are a number of restrictions and requirements of which managers should be aware before deciding whether or not to establish a UCITS. These include:

- restrictions on permitted assets

- concentration limits

- counterparty exposure limits

- limits on risk exposure / leverage

- restrictions on short selling

- collateral management obligations

- liquidity requirements

These need to be carefully evaluated and considered by any manager contemplating an absolute return UCITS. A number of strategies, including less liquid, highly leveraged or highly concentrated strategies, will not be suitable.

## 7. HEDGE FUND OFFERING TERMS

The terms upon which interests in a hedge fund are issued to investors define both the commercial terms upon which investors participate in investment returns and the rights of investors in respect to their investment.

The nature of the interests held by an investor in a hedge fund will reflect the legal form of the fund. For example, investors in a fund established as a body corporate will generally be issued with shares in the fund and have the status of shareholder; investors in a unit trust will generally be issued with units (representing a beneficial interest) in the trust and have the status of unit holder; and investors in a limited partnership will be issued with limited partnership interests (generally representing a capital account in the name of the investor) in the limited partnership and have the status of limited partner.

The precise voting and other rights granted to the investor are set out in the constitutional documents of the fund. In common with many other types of funds, investors tend to participate in hedge fund structures through multiple share classes (and, sometimes, series within a class). The need for multiple share classes (and multiple series of a class) reflects the regulatory and operational requirements of the fund itself. However, multiple classes are also required to give effect to the different terms upon which investors participate in the fund profits.

## Accumulation/Distribution Policy

A typical hedge fund will adopt an accumulation or "roll up" policy. In such circumstances the fund does not seek to distribute net income or capital profits, whether by way of dividends (in the case of a fund in corporate form) or distributions (in the case of a limited partnership or unit trust). Instead, profits are retained within the fund and reinvested as part of its ongoing investment strategy.

As a result, the standard approach is to issue to investors accumulation (i.e. non-distribution/dividend paying) shares or interests. This is also consistent with the tax requirements of many types of investor, particularly those who invest in a hedge fund via a non tax-transparent entity. Such investors may prefer not to realise a tax event until their interests in the relevant fund are redeemed/withdrawn (and thus any investment gain is realised).

There are circumstances, however, where it may be appropriate to structure the fund so as to pay distributions by way of dividend or similar arrangement. Some of these circumstances are outlined below.

## Funding Tax Charges

Certain categories of investor can be subject to tax on the underlying income or gains of the hedge fund as they arise. This is more typical of investors in tax-transparent structures. It is usually less of an issue for investors in non tax-transparent structures who are generally only taxed when they realise their interest in the fund; although it should be noted that certain categories of investor can still be treated as subject to tax on the underlying activities of a corporate fund.

Typically a hedge fund will permit relatively regular redemptions and investors who are taxed on a transparent basis in relation to the underlying profits and income of the fund will be able to help fund tax charges in this way. However, in circumstances where:

(i)     a hedge fund strategy is relatively illiquid and, as a result, redemptions of interests are limited or restricted; or

(ii)   the hedge fund imposes long "lock up" periods on investors during which redemptions are not permitted,

it may be important to offer investors the option of receiving regular distributions and/or dividends through holding distributing interests in a fund. Often, this is linked to the net income generated by the fund's portfolio. However, sometimes dividend and/or distribution rights are required to be extended to cover some part of the capital profits of the fund.

**Reporting Fund Status**

Under the UK's offshore fund tax rules, any gains realised by a UK taxable individual investor on the redemption or disposal of an interest in an offshore fund will be treated as "offshore income gains" subject to income tax at up to 45% (rather than capital gains at a maximum rate of 20%) unless the relevant fund (or share class) is approved by HM Revenue & Customs as a "reporting fund". Approval as a reporting fund requires the relevant fund (or share class) to 'report' income to UK investors in respect of each accounting period, with such investors being taxable on their share of such reported income (even if no income is actually distributed).

In overview, if the fund is likely to generate significant capital gains and is targeting UK individual investors or other classes of investor for whom capital gains treatment is favourable (such as UK authorised funds and investments trusts which are exempt from tax on capital gains), the fund may wish to consider seeking approval as a reporting fund (which can be done on a class by class basis).

**Liquidity and Return of Capital Policy**

A hedge fund which invests in an asset class which is highly liquid will generally be expected to offer regular dealing days upon which

172

investors may subscribe for interests in the fund and/or redeem their shares subject to providing specified notice.

A fund whose strategy is less liquid may wish to limit the redemption rights it offers (for example, by reducing the regularity of dealing days, increasing notice periods or requiring investors to accept hard or soft lock up periods).

AIFMD requires managers to ensure consistency between the investment strategy, liquidity profile and redemption policy.

## Base Currency of Account and Currency Classes

In common with other types of fund, the currency in which a fund is valued and in which it reports its performance is important to investors and the manager. A fund whose investments are largely traded or valued in a particular currency (such as US dollars or euro) may choose to value its portfolio and report its performance in that currency. This is usually termed the "base currency" or "currency of account" of the fund. Where a fund is exposed to multiple currencies, the chosen base currency tends to be the primary currency to which the performance of the fund is exposed although sometimes managers will adopt a base currency which equates to the currency in which investors are primarily invested in the fund.

Hedge funds often include, as part of their investment strategy, efficient portfolio management powers entitling the manager to enter into forward foreign exchange and derivative transactions to hedge against or mitigate the risk of adverse foreign exchange movements between the fund's base currency and the currencies to which its underlying assets are exposed. Such provisions can also be extended to permit the manager to hedge other potential exposures, including interest rate and other macro and micro risks. The costs, profits and/or losses attributable to such transactions are generally borne by all the investors in the fund.

Many hedge funds offer investors the opportunity of investing in multiple currencies (i.e. currencies other than the base currency of account) represented by different classes or series of shares or interests in the fund. The value of such classes will be affected (positively as well as negatively) by foreign exchange movements between the currency of the relevant class and the fund's base currency and underlying currency exposures. Hedge fund terms often entitle the manager to conduct hedging transactions in relation to the relevant share class. The costs, profits and/or losses attributable to such transactions are generally borne by the relevant currency class and the investors invested in that class.

**New Issues**

A fund may need to have separate classes for persons who can and those who cannot invest in "new issues", which is a US concept.

"New issues" are initial public offerings ("IPOs") of securities made pursuant to a registration statement or offering circular. As a general rule, members of the US Financial Industry Regulatory Authority ("FINRA") are prohibited from selling to restricted persons[3], and restricted persons are not allowed to invest in new issues[4].

Accordingly, a fund wishing to invest in new issues may need to establish restricted and unrestricted classes of shares (for restricted

---

[3] The term "restricted person" generally includes any of the following: (i) broker-dealers; their officers, directors, general partners, associated persons and employees; their agents engaged in the investment banking or securities business; and their immediate family members, except for broker-dealers and their employees who limit their business to the purchase and sale of investment company, variable contract, or direct participation securities; and owners of a broker-dealer and their immediate family members; (ii) finders and fiduciaries and their immediate family members, but only with respect to initial public offerings in which they are involved; (iii) portfolio managers (e.g. any person with authority to buy or sell securities for an investment manager or any collective investment account (even if it is not the account for which the new issues are being purchased)) and their immediate family members.

[4] However, note that as an exception to the general rule, a fund which has restricted persons as investors can invest in new issues provided that the level of restricted persons investing in the fund does not exceed the threshold level of 10 per cent. of the beneficial interests of the fund.

and unrestricted persons) in order to allow unrestricted investors to participate in such new issues for so long as such securities remain new issues.

## Management Class

The manager, its personnel and their connected persons may wish to invest in the fund as a means of showing confidence in the hedge fund's objective and strategy through a 'management' class reserved for them (indeed it is usually expected that the lead portfolio manager invest in the fund so as to ensure an alignment of interests). Such management classes often benefit from lower or no management or performance fees or allocations but are otherwise generally subject to similar terms to other investor classes.

Management shares can also be utilised to vest in the management group the right to vote on key aspects of the fund such as changes to its constitution or the appointment of directors. Good market practice is generally to ensure that investors are still entitled to vote on any material changes or variations to their class rights to ensure their interests are protected.

## Fee Structure

One of the key aspects of the terms of issue of any hedge fund is fees. Hedge funds typically pay its appointed investment manager a management fee and a performance fee/allocation.

The management fee is generally paid monthly or quarterly and is calculated with reference to a specified annual percentage rate of the fund's net asset value. The annual percentage rate can vary between strategies, management groups and share classes. Generally speaking, the percentage rate is between 1 and 2 per cent. per annum.

The principle underlying a performance related fee or allocation (referred to here as a "performance fee") is that the investment manager should be incentivised as to, and rewarded for, its level of absolute performance calculated by reference to the net asset value of the fund over specified performance periods. Historically, performance periods have been 12 month periods ending on the annual accounting date of a fund, which is often set as 31 December in each year so as to tie in with US tax reporting. However, performance periods can be more or less frequent.

Given that the performance fee is calculated with regard to realised and unrealised profits of the fund (as reflected in its published net asset value), most hedge fund terms will provide for under performance in respect of an investor's holding in the fund to be carried forward so that performance fees are not paid twice in respect of the same performance. This is generally expressed in terms of a high water mark or 'loss carry forward'.

The two primary mechanisms used to ensure performance fees are not paid twice in respect of the same performance in a unitised structure are:

(a)     Equalisation accounting – equalisation is more common in European managed funds, although it is complex, difficult to apply without the appropriate computer programs and difficult to explain to investors. It involves investors paying an additional sum at the time of their investment equal to the existing accrual per share in respect of the performance fee where the fund is above its most recent high water mark (or, where an investor invests in the fund when the fund is below its most recent high water mark, to make provision for a partial share redemption to fund the performance fee in respect of any application of the net asset value up to the point where the high water mark is again reached). Dependent upon fund performance, the equalisation amount is subsequently returned to the investor (directly or via additional interests in the fund) or paid to the investment manager.

(b)  Series accounting – this methodology provides for the issuance of a new class (or series of a class) of shares as of each dealing date in respect of which shares are issued, which provides for a different net asset value for each series. This solution, traditionally more common in US managed funds but which is often also preferred by European managers, is relatively easy to understand and administer, and the results closely match partnership accounting with less complexity than equalisation accounting. However, where continuous losses arise numerous classes of series may be issued, which may give rise to administrative costs and burdens.

It is not unusual in hedge fund structures for promoters to offer multiple classes of share to which different levels of management fee and/or performance fee apply. Typically, such funds offer investorsthe opportunity of investing in regular share classes which are subject to standard liquidity terms (e.g. regular redemptions on monthly or quarterly redemption dealing days on thirty days' notice). As an alternative, investors may be permitted to invest in share classes which are subject to more constrained liquidity terms in return for more attractive (i.e. lower) rates of management and/or performance fees. Such classes may be subject to a minimum "lock-up" period during which redemptions are not permitted, longer notice periods and/or more limited redemption dealing days. They may also be subject to a higher minimum level of investment per investor. Variants can involve "softer" lock-up provisions whereby investors may redeem their shares before the expiry of the relevant lock-up period subject to the deduction of a fee from the redemption proceeds payable to the fund and/or the manager.

**Frequency of Dealing**

Hedge funds pursuing a reasonably liquid investment strategy will generally be expected by investors to permit the regular subscription and redemption of interests in the fund. Many will offer monthly or quarterly dealing days and require investors to give the fund not less than 30 days' prior written notice of redemption requests.

An investor subscribing or redeeming interests in the fund will generally do so at a subscription or redemption price calculated with respect to the net asset value of the fund. Subscriptions and redemptions tend to take effect as of specified dealing days on which banks in specified jurisdictions are open for business.

For less liquid strategies, funds can impose more constrained dealing terms. Examples include:

•       longer notice periods and/or a reduction in the frequency of dealing days;

•       hard lock provisions whereby investors are not permitted to redeem their interests for a specified "lock-up" period;

•       soft lock provisions whereby investors which redeem interests within the specified "lock-up" period are permitted to redeem but pay an "early redemption" charge set at a rate designed to incentivise investors to hold their interests for the full "soft lock" period and compensate continuing investors for the impact that the early redemption has on the fund; or

•       staged redemption provisions whereby investors submitting a redemption request have their interests realised over a number of dealing days.

**Managing Exceptional Circumstances**

In normal market conditions, requests for the redemption of interests should be given effect to as of the relevant dealing day and redemption proceeds calculated and paid in cash within a pre-agreed timeframe thereafter.

However, the governing body of a fund (e.g. the board of directors) may conclude that it is no longer possible or fair to all investors to satisfy redemptions in accordance with normal arrangements. In reaching such a conclusion, the governing body must have due regard to the interests of continuing investors as well as those seeking to redeem their interests. The governing body may reach such a view where, for example:

• due to liquidity concerns relating to the assets of the fund, it is not possible to easily realise those assets to provide cash to satisfy a redemption;

• as a result of realising liquid assets to satisfy redemption proceeds, the proportion of the fund's portfolio represented by less liquid assets would rise to a level which is not compatible with the investment strategy of the fund or would otherwise be unfair to continuing investors;

• assets are likely to be realised at prices detrimental to investors (which may include both redeeming and continuing investors, depending on timing);

• taking into account the legitimate cash requirements of the fund, the fund would be prevented from meeting its continuing obligations and maintain a solvent position; or

• the fund is subject to other events which may affect its ability to satisfy redemption requests (such as political or economic factors affecting its ability to trade in certain markets or to repatriate or transfer moneys).

If it is concluded that it is not appropriate to meet redemptions on a given dealing day in full on a cash basis, then the fund's governing body should have in place sufficient liquidity management arrangements at its disposal to be able to manage the situation effectively and fairly. Such arrangements should be properly disclosed to investors in the information memorandum of the fund. Arrangements of this nature typically include:

• Gates

A gate is a mechanism whereby the redemption of interests may be limited on a particular dealing day to a stated maximum (usually a percentage of the interests in issue or of the net asset value in the fund, or a particular class, or an investor's total holding in the fund), in circumstances where the governing body believes that such an action would be in the overall best interests of investors. To the extent redemption requests are not satisfied on a given dealing day, unsatisfied requests are then carried forward to future dealing days.

This may be a reasonable approach if the deferral of the timing of redemptions of interests is likely to enable the fund to meet redemptions thereafter. However, if priority (on subsequent dealing days) is given to investors whose redemption requests are carried forward, there is a risk that all remaining investors will seek to submit redemption requests immediately in order to avoid having their rights to redeem being effectively subordinated.

An alternative is to provide that unsatisfied redemption requests carried forward do not have priority but will be redeemed pro rata with other outstanding redemption requests.

- Satisfying redemption proceeds in specie or in kind

Many private investment funds include provisions permitting redemption proceeds to be satisfied by the transfer to the investor of assets of the fund having an equivalent value as determined in accordance with the normal valuation provisions of the fund (a redemption in specie).

- Side pockets

Side pockets are often used as a mechanism for a fund to separate assets or positions that have become illiquid and/or hard to value from the fund's general portfolio. The relevant assets are managed and realised as a separate pool either within the fund (in which case they tend to be represented by a separate class of interests in the fund issued to investors) or are transferred to a separate liquidating vehicle.

The attraction of a side pocket arrangement is that all investors of record at the time of imposition of the side pocket participate in the side pocket whilst subsequent investors in the fund do not.

Historically, side pockets have tended to be used to deal with assets which have become hard to value and where a decision has been taken to write down their value in the books of the fund. By using a side pocket, investors of record who have borne the write down are able to take advantage of any future recovery in the value of the asset(s) rather than subsequent subscribers acquiring that opportunity at an undervalue at the expense of those investors.

- Suspension of Dealing

The ultimate sanction available to the governing body of a fund is to suspend redemptions.

It is long-established practice for the terms of issue of all open-ended funds to include provisions permitting such a suspension in a range of circumstances.

The terms of issue of most hedge funds also permit the governing body to suspend the calculation of the fund's net asset value (which may in turn necessitate a general suspension of subscriptions and redemptions).

## PART 3 – FUND MANAGER STRUCTURING CONSIDERATIONS

*LLP OR LIMITED COMPANY*

UK investment management businesses are typically established as limited liability partnerships ("LLPs") or private limited companies. The appropriate choice of vehicle will depend upon the specific circumstances and should be considered on a case by case basis.

## KEY CORPORATE TAX FEATURES

For corporate law purposes, both LLPs and limited companies are limited liability bodies corporate, meaning the liability of the owners of the business (whether members of an LLP or shareholders in a limited company) for the debts of the entity are limited to their capital contributions to the business.

Limited companies are treated as tax opaque corporate entities for tax purposes. A company will therefore be subject to UK corporation tax on its profits. The principals of an investment management business will typically be shareholders of the company, in which capacity they will ultimately control the company and may be entitled to receive dividends. They may also be employees and/or directors of the company, in which capacity they will perform services for the company and may be entitled to remuneration in the form of salary and bonus.

In contrast, LLPs are treated as tax transparent partnerships for tax purposes. The principals of an investment management business will be members (partners) in the LLP and self-employed for tax purposes. Since the LLP is tax transparent, it will not be subject to tax. Instead, the members of the LLP will be treated as carrying on the business and will be taxable directly on their share of the LLP's profits. The members of an LLP will agree how to share income and capital in the LLP's governing documentation.

## HISTORIC USE

For a number of years, LLPs have been the preferred management vehicle of the UK investment management industry. However, following changes to tax legislation in recent years, some new entrants into the investment management industry are giving additional consideration to establishing their businesses as limited liability companies rather than LLPs.

## USING AN LLP

Some of the potential advantages of using an LLP relative to a limited company are:

•       Members of an LLP are generally (though not always) treated as self-employed for tax purposes. They receive their income by way of profit share rather than by salary and bonus. This can lead to a significant tax saving for the business, since employers' National Insurance Contributions ("NICs") are not generally due on profit share (but would be payable on salary and bonus if they were employees). The current rate of employers' NICs is 13.8%.

•       As partners are taxed on their share of partnership profits, where there are no profits (for example in the early years of a business) a partner will not be subject to tax in the relevant tax year even if they receive partnership drawings (although they may be subject to tax on such amounts in later tax years).

•       LLPs are very flexible and enable new members to be added without incurring a tax charge (which may not be the case with limited companies). They also allow the profit and capital sharing rights of the members to be adjusted by agreement, with no need to adjust shareholdings (which can lead to additional tax in a corporate structure).

•    Although dependent on personal tax circumstances, for a UK resident individual who pays income tax at the highest rate of tax, receiving a share of LLP profits may be marginally more tax efficient than receiving dividends from a UK company after the company has paid corporation tax.

•    LLPs may offer a more collegiate atmosphere than a company. Individuals typically welcome the status of being a "partner" in the business and this may assist with the recruitment and retention of staff.

•    Since members of LLPs do not have employment rights, LLPs may offer greater contractual certainty in connection with the removal of members and the enforcement of restrictive covenants following their departure. In contrast, principals of a limited company investment management business will be directors and/or employees of the company. Employment rights may make it more difficult or costly for the company to remove individual employees and/or enforce any restrictive covenants following their departures.

•    Unlike employee shareholders of companies, members of an LLP will not automatically be subject to the UK's complex employment related security tax regime (although this regime may still be a relevant consideration in structuring). Broadly, these rules can potentially impose income tax (and NICs) liabilities each time employees acquire (or dispose of) shares for less than (or more than) market value by reason of their employment (whether the shares are in the limited company or another vehicle, such as a fund).

•    The employment related security rules which apply to companies can make it difficult to award equity to employees or to adjust the principals' respective shareholdings in the company. This makes an LLP more flexible than a limited company in terms of bringing in new equity holders or adjusting profit shares.

*USING A LIMITED COMPANY:*

Some of the potential advantages of using a limited company relative to an LLP are:

• Limited companies are typically simpler and cheaper to establish and maintain whereas LLPs can be more time consuming and costly to establish and operate.

• Individual members of an LLP wishing to reinvest profits into the business must do so after paying income tax. In contrast, profits can be reinvested in a limited company structure after incurring corporation tax (at materially lower corporation tax rates than income tax rates). The rate is currently 20%, reducing to 19% in April 2017 and 17% in April 2020. This allows shareholders in a limited company to reinvest profits in the business more efficiently than is the case for members of an LLP.

• For a non-UK resident individual it may be possible to avoid further UK tax on dividends paid by a company. This benefit can also be relevant for a UK resident individual who intends to become non-UK resident in the future, provided that dividends are deferred within that time.

• Unlike a partner with self-employed status, a director of a company will have employment law rights.

Finally, under current legislation, employees and directors of a company may be outside the scope of the new income based carried interest rules, potentially making it easier to achieve capital gains tax on carried interest.

In addition to the UK corporate structure, there may well be one or more non-UK entities in the management group, either as holding or operating entities.

The regulatory status of the UK manager will also need careful consideration, including whether it is to be an "Alternative Investment Fund Manager", or operate under the "MiFID" regime.

Such considerations will form a key part of the initial business structuring discussions, but are outside the scope of this chapter.


## PART 4 – SEEDING AND ACCELERATION DEALS


### INTRODUCTION

Whilst the larger and more established seeders do have their own 'standard' terms, there is no such thing as a 'standard' seed deal. Seeding deals can vary widely, from seed investors who require preferential investment terms, to seed investors who require control over the constitution of the fund and its offering terms together with a share of future revenues and/or an equity stake in the investment management business. In return, the fund manager should secure a significant amount of seed capital which should effectively cover its operating costs for the initial period of its life. Break even asset levels are now much higher and third party seed capital is often key to a new manager launching a viable business.

Seed deals should be distinguished from 'early bird' or seed share classes which are often offered to initial stage investors. These classes will usually bear lower fee rates, often in return for a longer lock-up period and perhaps a higher minimum investment amount – but there is no separate 'seed deal' as such. The availability of these classes is often limited to a specified investment amount and/or time period.

Depending on the terms of the deal, seeders might also provide working capital to the investment management business together with business support, whether that be the sharing of resources (in particular with the marketing and distribution of the fund) or simply providing guidance on how to run a successful investment management business. Reputable seed investors also offer a 'stamp of approval' along with introductions to other investors, which can help the seeded fund grow.

A list of early-stage backers of hedge funds is given in Chapter 12.

Whilst seeding deals help ensure that a hedge fund launch is viable, care needs to be taken to ensure that it does not materially prejudice the long term viability of the fund and the investment management business. Prospective investors may be put off by a fund with high investor concentration and with one key investor exercising significant control over the fund and management business. There is a balance to be struck.


## PREFERENTIAL TERMS OF INVESTMENT

The following is a high level overview of some of the key terms often seen in seed deals as pertains to the seeder's fund investment.

**Management Fee.** A seed investor will seek a lower management fee than that paid by ordinary investors. In order to support the manager in its formative years, management fees may be charged on a sliding scale depending on the amount invested (whereby a higher management fee is payable by the seed investor whilst the fund is small with the management fee decreasing as the fund reaches a viable size).

**Performance Fee.** The seed investor will also usually pay a lower performance fee in respect of its investment in the fund, perhaps depending on the amount of capital it has allocated to the deal.

**Transparency and Information Rights**. The seed investor will likely require transparency and access to certain information that a manager would not otherwise offer to investors. This might include regular performance and risk reporting, position level transparency and access to third parties so as to verify the information provided.

**Limits on Concentration and Leverage**. The seed investor might specify certain limits on the fund's investment strategy. The limits might include (i) overall portfolio notional limits (gross, long and short), (ii) overall portfolio risk limits, (iii) initial margin limits, (iv) individual security limits, (v) geographic limits and (vi) non-equity limits. A manager should seek to ensure that any such restrictions do not impact on its ability to achieve the fund's stated investment objective and strategy.

**Founder Investment.** The seed investor will often require that the founder make and maintain a minimum investment in the fund. Such amounts vary widely. Often the founder is not entitled to withdraw his investment until after the end of the seed investor's lock-up period.

**Additional Investments**. A seed investor is often granted the right to make additional investments in the fund on the same terms as the initial investment (or to introduce others who invest on similarly favourable terms). The right often extends to other investment funds established by the investment manager.  If the capacity of the fund's strategy is limited, a manager should consider how much it will allow to be utilised on such less remunerative arrangements.

**Additional Fund Investors**.  The seed investor might specify the dealing terms upon which other investors will invest in the fund (for example, minimum investment amounts, management fees and performance fees and redemption rights).

**Devotion of Time.** The founder is usually required to devote substantially all of his business time and attention to the affairs of the fund and the investment management business. If he ceases to do so, the seed investor usually has the right to redeem. The founder might be required to agree not to undertake any personal account dealing.

**Approval Rights.** The seed investor might seek approval rights in respect of the fund, including pre-approval of: (i) any material amendment to the material fund documents, including any material change to the investment strategy and process; (ii) the appointment of key service providers; and (iii) the offering of more favourable terms to other investors.

**MFN.** The seed investor often includes a "most-favoured nations" clause in any seed deal meaning that it must also be offered any preferential term offered to another investor. This is aimed at preventing another investor from receiving better terms of investment.

**Gates.** The seed investor might request that it has veto rights over the imposition of any fund or investor level gate, albeit this should be resisted if possible. A compromise might be for this veto right to exist for so long as the seed investor holds more than a certain percentage of the fund interests in issue.

**Redemption Rights.** The seed investor's initial investment will likely be subject to a lock-up period, typically between 2 to 3 years but it may be longer depending on the fund's strategy.

*REVENUE SHARING ARRANGEMENTS*

A significant seed investor will often seek a certain percentage of any management fees and performance fees received from third party investment in the fund. If a fund is successful, the return from these revenue sharing arrangements can be significant.

A deal based on gross revenues received by the manager is generally easier to document and negotiate than a deal based on net income or net profits. In the latter case, the seeder will need to maintain a certain amount of control over the expenditure of the management business and will require transparency rights over accounts and financial statements and approval rights over budgets or exceptional items.

The right to receive a share of revenues might cease once the seeder redeems from the fund. Alternatively, the right might continue for a certain period of time following the seed investor's redemption (or perhaps indefinitely). An exit strategy should be agreed at the outset (see further "Exit Arrangements" below).


*EQUITY IN THE INVESTMENT MANAGEMENT BUSINESS*


A significant seed investor might also look to take an equity stake in the management business, usually in return for the injection of working capital. An equity stake will usually allow the seed investor to benefit from the sale of the investment management business.

Where a loan is advanced, a relatively low amount of interest is usually charged and the loan obligation is often secured against future revenues.

In the event of a revenue sharing arrangement and/or the granting of any equity stake in the investment management business, the seed investor will likely require a certain level of control and transparency over the business. This might include:

**Annual Budget.** The seed investor might have pre-approval rights over the investment management business' budgets.

**Compensation Limitations.** The seed investor might seek to restrict the compensation of the founder and other staff of the investment manager.

**Issuance of Further Equity.** The founder might be required to obtain prior approval from the seed investor before issuing any further equity in the investment management business. In these circumstances, the founder should look to carve out a right to issue up to a certain amount of equity without prior approval. The founder should also ensure that it has appropriate flexibility to grow the business through the issuance of equity to new business partners. In the event new equity is issued, the founder should seek to ensure that the seed investor is subject to a pro-rata dilution (otherwise the seed investor might disproportionately benefit from any growth in the business).

**Approvals.** The seed investor might seek approval rights in respect of the management business, including: (i) any material amendment to the management group's material documents; (ii) the payment of dividends and distributions; (iii) the merger or consolidation of any entity of the investment management business with, or sale of substantially all of its assets to, any other person or entity; (iv) the launch of any additional funds managed by the founder or the investment management business; (v) dissolution of the fund or any entity of the investment management business; (vi) any loans made to or by an entity in the investment management business (other than in the ordinary course of business); and (vii) the entering into any onerous obligation outside the ordinary course of business.

**Non-Compete.** The founder will likely be under an obligation not to compete with the investment management business upon his departure (for a certain period of time, say 12 to 24 months).

*EXIT ARRANGEMENTS*

Arrangements should be put in place for an agreed exit strategy between the parties. For example, the rights of the seed investor may terminate upon the seed investment in the fund being withdrawn (or after a certain period of time thereafter) and/or may be subject to buy out rights in favour of the founder (linked to multiples of revenues or valuations).

The seed investor might seek a tag along right such that, if the founder desires to sell all or any portion of his interests in the investment management business, the seed investor will also be granted the right to sell all or the pro rata share of its interests in the investment management business on the same economic terms and conditions.

The founder should seek to place restrictions on the transfer of the seed investor's interest in the investment management business. It is common for the seed investor to be precluded from transferring its interest for a certain period (for example during the lock up period). Following the expiry of the lock-up period, the founder's right to transfer its interest might be subject to a pre-emption right whereby the founder has the right of first refusal or first offer. It is also common for the seed investor to agree not to transfer interests to any third-party who would be objectionable to the founder (for example, a competitor).

PART 5 – SELECTING A LEGAL SERVICES PROVIDER, INCLUDING SUGGESTED KEY QUESTIONS

## WHAT MAKES DECHERT LLC THE LAW FIRM OF CHOICE FOR HEDGE FUNDS?

Dechert is recognised internationally as the leading legal adviser for the hedge fund industry. It is the firm of choice for many of the world's largest hedge fund and emerging fund managers seeking comprehensive, cross-border service.

Dechert remains the only law firm with a physical presence in all of Europe's key fund jurisdictions including London, Dublin, Luxembourg, Paris and Munich/Frankfurt in addition to offices elsewhere in Europe, the Middle East, United States and Asia. Our European footprint means we are uniquely placed to advise across a range of products and options available to hedge fund managers including the relative merits of European and offshore funds and the offering of alternative strategies through retail products as well as the impact of AIFMD on manager group structures. More recently we have helped clients on more hybrid structures which share hedge and private equity type characteristics, and the strength in depth in both our hedge fund and private equity practices means we are well placed to support clients in this area.

Chambers UK has ranked Dechert in the top tier for investment funds: hedge funds for ten consecutive years. Hedge Fund Journal recently voted Dechert the "Leading European Practice – London, Dublin, Luxembourg, Frankfurt and Paris" at the Hedge Fund Journal Awards, 2017. In addition, Dechert was recognised as the "Best Onshore Law Firm for Hedge Fund Start-Ups" at the HMF Awards 2016.


## KEY QUESTIONS TO ASK A POTENTIAL LAWYER

What experience does your firm have in establishing hedge funds and hedge fund managers (including with a strategy similar to the one we intend to pursue)? Please provide details of recent experience and references.

Do you have a US presence and is your firm able to assist with US regulatory and US tax issues 'in house'? Do you have US qualified lawyers based in London?

Do you have offices in Europe's key fund jurisdictions, including Dublin and Luxembourg? Can your firm provide impartial advice on the most suitable domicile for our fund, be it 'offshore' Cayman or 'onshore' Europe?

What experience do you have in negotiating seed deals? Please provide examples of recent deal experience.

In light of recent pressure on hedge fund fees, what experience do you have in structuring alternative management and performance fee arrangements? Please provide examples.

Do you have experience in negotiating trading documentation and service provider contracts with the leading hedge fund prime brokers and administrator/depositary service providers? Please provide details of recent experience and volume.

Is your firm able to help us navigate the regulatory requirements applicable to marketing the fund on a global basis?

Are you able to offer a full legal service to the fund and the fund management business both during and following establishment (for example, can you provide support in the areas of intellectual property, real estate, employment, tax, finance, corporate and litigation)?

How do you keep clients up to date with relevant legal and regulatory developments? Do you circulate regular newsletters and legal updaters and what seminars and conferences do you hold?

How does your firm seek to provide hedge fund and fund management clients with added value? What distinguishes your firm from your competitors?

## CONTACT INFORMATION

Dechert LLP

**Primary Contact:** Gus Black, Partner

gus.black@dechert.com

+44 20 7184 7380

**Alternative Contact:** Craig Borthwick, Senior Associate

craig.borthwick@dechert.com

+44 20 7184 7631

Switchboard: +44 20 7184 7000

**Website:** www.dechert.com

**Address:** 160 Queen Victoria Street, London EC4V 4QQ

# CHAPTER 9. IT SERVICES & CONSULTANCY FOR HEDGE FUNDS

## By Tom Woollard of Edge Technology Group

## About the author

*Tom Woollard is Managing Director for the European & Asia Operations of Edge Technology Group "ETG". Mr Woollard has been advising Financial Services firms from Greenfield start-up to multi-billion dollar investment managers at Director and CTO Levels since 2005. Having represented start-up firms and established firms alike, in addition to working directly for firms with varying strategies, Mr Woollard has unique hands-on experience of working with C–Level staff to help build IT Infrastructure, policies, and platforms, in-line with the requirements of their business at the varying stages of evolution during their lifecycle, including complex and difficult wind-up scenarios. ETG extended their operation to the Europe region with a London HQ in the summer of 2011, after an introduction between Mr Woollard and ETG's founding partner and CEO, Jim Nekos. Mr Nekos has been working within Financial Services since the early 1990's and has extensive experience within the securities industry. Such experience includes senior positions at MS Prime Brokerage, PB Execution, Barclays Capital Prime Brokerage, and Daiwa Securities. The mutual respect and shared work ethic between Mr Woollard and Mr Nekos has seen the Global firm at Edge grow in each of their respective regions and expand throughout Asia in more recent times.*

## About Edge Technology Group

Edge Technology Group is a Fully Managed IT Service Provider, Consultancy and Advisory operation with offices and Datacentres based throughout Europe, The

Americas, and Asia. ETG is a purpose-built collective group of Global ex-Hedge Fund CTO's, exclusively put together to represent firms within the financial services sector. Edge follows a common blueprint in each of our respective global offices with ex Hedge Fund CTO's and COO's running each regional office whilst attracting and retaining the services of leading Hedge Fund IT industry professionals to represent the firm as its support and engineering personnel. It is very much a "Know your product. Know your audience" approach to outsourced IT services. A white glove service delivery model specifically designed to meet the 24 hour nature of financial services firm. This approach to service excellence has helped our firm maintain an extremely loyal list of clientele with extremely high client and staff retention. Our work ethic is very much in line with that of our client base and we are therefore able to extend a single entity mind-set to each and every one of our clients.

## WHAT DOES AN IT SERVICE PROVIDER DO FOR A START-UP HEDGE FUND?

During a hedge fund firm's inception phase, the best stage to bring in an IT service provider is quite simply, as early as possible. Involving a firm even before the requirements of an infrastructure platform are specified, your trusted IT partner can help in an advisory capacity - helping you with Due Diligence Agendas, governing body application processes, site surveys on potential office spaces, vendor management and due diligence, and the formation of documentation and policy sets, to name but a few of the benefits. It is also an opportunity for the Client and the Service Provider to build a true partnership, and begin to understand how one another operate.

Prior to the 2008 financial crisis, having a CTO, reflecting a bias to In-House expertise, was extremely common, and very much the preferred model within financial services firms, and amongst Hedge Funds in particular. Whilst that model is still very common among the larger firms managing multi-billion dollar assets and multiple geographic locations, there has been a shift in that pattern throughout the sector and across firms of varying size, such that outsourcing the management of IT infrastructure and all of the common tasks typically associated with the role of a CTO has increased. This is particularly true for start-ups. This usually led to one of two common outcomes: where there was more proprietary infrastructure and the CTO has a development background the firms stayed with the status quo, where the technology was more vanilla/industry standard external service providers became involved. This trend came at a time when Virtual IT Infrastructure was considered mature technology and widely utilised by financial services firms.

In addition to post launch requirements, IT service providers can get involved with new hedge fund firms at varying stages of their inception period. This covers the range from working in an advisory capacity for firms yet to even register their entity to firms that have already secured significant seed capital, and are looking to build investor grade and governing body compliant IT Infrastructure with immediate effect.

Your IT service provider can:

- Build investor-grade and governing-body-compliant IT Infrastructure from day 1.

- Help the fund manager through the due diligence process as far as technology infrastructure, support, and disaster recovery, are concerned.

You should be aware that investors in hedge funds are looking for three attributes in the technology implemented: scalability, security, and high availability.

When comparing the role of an outsourced IT Service Provider to years gone by, 2017 is a very good time to launch a Hedge Fund when working in partnership with a service provider. IT Infrastructure systems have vastly matured in the areas of networking, storage, and virtualisation technologies, which means that most credible IT service providers can offer start-up firms incredibly robust, highly-available, and scalable systems for day-1 operation. This is especially true when cloud computing is considered.

Governing Body rules and regulations have also vastly changed in recent times and as a result, service providers have often been put under the spotlight, particularly as part of 3rd party or investor due diligence agenda's. Because of such changes and the risk associated with leveraging service providers, all reputable firms will have offerings that have been built to ensure that they are tailored to meet the requirements of such regulation and scrutiny.


**Cloud Services**

There is still mixed opinion about the benefit of public cloud versus private cloud services. "Understandably so, as there are a broad range of services that can be implemented under the guise of "the cloud". In this section, we are going to address the provision of private cloud services, such as ETG's Fully Managed IT platform, "Edge HFB", our Infrastructure as a Services (IaaS) product.

In our opinion, for firms working within the financial services sector, we very much believe that you should only ever consider a private cloud platform, although we appreciate that public cloud environments are maturing quickly and getting more and more viable within our vertical. Our interpretation of a private cloud platform is an IT Infrastructure that is purpose built on a client-by-client basis and delivered as a service directly to the client via the Outsourced IT providers own Datacentres over stable and redundant leased-line connections. A private cloud platform such as Edge HFB, means that your environment is entirely isolated and dedicated to yourself as a customer, entirely secure, and supported as a front-to-back solution by engineers in direct employment by the IT service provider. The service provider effectively therefore owns and manages every single element of the delivery of this platform and can therefore guarantee Service Level Agreements (SLAs) in-line with your business requirements.

The same cannot be said for Public Cloud services. Public Cloud services that are often seen as an equivalent to the above are services such as Microsoft Office 365 and Google Docs, and leveraging other public services such as Dropbox for shared corporate files. The costs of such services are of course far more competitive/cheaper than those of a privately delivered platform and we are often asked if we would support them as an alternative. Whilst such services are perfectly adequate and respectable services for the provision of IT Infrastructure to most organisations in a production environment, we simply believe they have a *limited* place in the financial services sector for reasons of quality and assurance of it. A service provider such as ourselves, could never guarantee SLA's around the service and support of such products as they are completely out of our control and management jurisdiction. Historically, they would also raise serious concerns as part of 3rd party and investor due diligence. I say historically as at the time of writing, such products are absolutely making their own investments to ensure they are far more compliant and secure than when they first came to market. Infrastructure is absolutely a commodity and very much like water from a tap, Infrastructure can be provisioned at the click of a button, both in the public and private cloud space. Commercially, the attraction of the public cloud appeals to many. You can also now partner with 3rd party security brokers that will provide a compliance wrapper around such public services. In addition to firms like ours, that will add a managed services wrapper (support, management, monitoring, Security etc) around such adaptations. Ultimately, we see a hybrid approach becoming more of the norm, i.e. firms will leverage a combination of the public and private cloud in addition to local on-premise resources to truly provide an environment or adaption of technology that works for them as a firm. The beauty of the cloud is, you have the flexibility to do whatever you choose, within varying scale of budgetary requirements.

Having worked within the industry at CTO level, Edge appreciates the value of time to market, defined deliverables and high availability and we therefore add value beyond simply providing you with an IT platform. We monitor the platform 24x7x365, we have staff that are familiar with not only your IT Infrastructure but your own staff and vendors, and we are able to give you high level or detailed insight about your IT Infrastructure at any point in time. Will you ever have IT issues on our platform? Of course you will. But we will be able to resolve them quickly and efficiently within agreed SLA's, and provide Reason for Outages (RFO's) thereafter. We will explain and highlight the cause, describe the remedy, and provide a long term solution to ensure it does not happen again. This level of service provision we consider a key ingredient, and it is missing from most public services.

At Edge, we launched our own cloud platform in November of 2007. Over that period-to-date, we have seen a huge shift in industry opinion toward cloud based services. What was once seen as a potential concern is now widely accepted and regarded as the de facto option for start-up Hedge Fund managers. In an established financial services firm, a true enterprise IT Infrastructure is built with high availability, redundancy, scale, and automation at the forefront of the design. To build an on-premise IT Infrastructure with all of those enterprise considerations from day 1 would cost a start-up manager of less than 50 people, tens of thousands of pounds in capital expenditure. That is before the management overhead of maintaining such systems has even been considered. Furthermore, to build such an IT Infrastructure at such expense for a relatively lean headcount at launch would often mean that you only ever use 10-30% capacity of that Infrastructure. By the time you start to really leverage the platform at closer to 60-70% utilisation, 3 or more years may have passed and the time to refresh certain components within the Infrastructure may be on the horizon, forcing you into another considerable outlay as hardware reaches end of life or is replaced with better performing systems.

One of the reasons start-up managers choose to leverage cloud computing at launch and one of the reasons it is widely recommended is that to do so, you would pay next to nothing in capital expenditure (although you should still budget for on premise equipment such as PC's and accessories, printers, LAN technology and connectivity) you would manage your IT expenditure in simple monthly payments to the Outsource IT service provider for the rental of an IT Infrastructure platform that is very much in-line with those seen on-premise within larger Hedge Fund Managers.

Given that in the setting-up phase there are only expenses, a reason for using cloud-based provision is that it turns capital outlays into (effectively) leasing arrangements, which will make cash-flows less negative in the period until fee income comes in.

To leverage the cloud also eliminates all proximity risks associated with your main premise of operation. If you leverage the cloud, any on premise issues in your office such as power cuts or any other loss of local service has absolutely no bearing on the performance of your production IT systems. They remain online, safe, and available, in a secure Datacentre, and it can very much promote the mobility of your workforce. That is such an arrangement could be considered part of your disaster-recovery plans, as well as facilitating remote working.

In our case our services are divided into five:

| Hedge Fund in a Box (HFB) | Disaster Recovery & Business Consultancy | Support Services | CTO Advisory | Security |
|---|---|---|---|---|
| Decades of cumulative experience building institutional-grade technology architectures for Hedge Funds. | Clients have zero downtime tolerance We get it. We offer customised solutions to address any RPO/RTO. | Remotely, ad hoc or dedicated on-site support services designed to act as an extension of your existing staff, proactively supporting your workforce. | Born from a networking group of ex-Hedge Fund CTOs, Edge can provide CTO-level assistance for any business requirement. | Security should not be considered as a hot-spot of today but as an ever evolving requirement at the forefront of design. |

## Ongoing Support

Infrastructure is so readily available now in many different forms that on-going support, and more importantly, *quality* on-going support, is often the main differentiator when choosing a service provider and IT Partner. At Edge, we pride ourselves on our support. For us, a successful support operation is as much about familiarity as it is about technical expertise and both are important in equal measure. Whilst technical expertise is of course paramount, all firms and businesses utilise their Infrastructure and system resource in very different ways. In an outsource model, support should therefore remain as personal and familiar as possible.

To have a team of experts that know your staff as much as your Infrastructure is very important as it helps to build trust within the relationship beyond the simple uptime and SLA's associated with your Infrastructure. At Edge, all of our support staff are industry recognised and directly employed, valued members of the global Edge business. Each technician is an industry professional used to the specific challenges and business issues arising in the financial sector, and asset management specifically. Employing staff directly from the industry means that staff are familiar with not only business-as-usual systems, but almost all typical financial services applications including many Portfolio Management Systems (PMS) and Order Management Systems (OMS). Staff retention and client familiarity help us maintain very high SLA's 24x7x365. When utilising Edge for support services, you will have access to a dedicated account manager, team leader, and dedicated support team. With an extremely low staff turnover of less than 1% since inception, maintaining tenure among our workforce gives our clientele familiarity among their outsourced support staff and further enhances the quality of the service you receive.

## Outsourced CTO

At Edge, our partner team acted in a direct Chief Technology Officer (CTO) capacity since the late 1990's. We have done this for firms ranging from start-up managers to $10 billion AUM-plus hedge funds. We have acted as advisors to the respective executive boards during periods of change – changes in regulation, increased assets and operational demands, client redemptions, and wind up scenarios. Edge has acted as architects and engineers when building internal IT platforms for firms implementing a range of strategies, including those with a high-end technology requirement, such as High Frequency Trading, quantitative, and proprietary strategies.

"Whether working remotely on an ad hoc basis or working as a dedicated resource on-site at your office, Edge support services are designed to act as an extension of your own staff, proactively supporting your workforce."

Much like IT Infrastructure, we have seen a shift to outsourced CTO in recent times. The CTO used to be one of the very first hires made by a start-up firm, and larger, more established, firms continue to operate the In-House CTO model. It is different for small and medium sized businesses.

Typically referred to as "The Virtual CTO", services can now be acquired from individuals and or firms, to provide CTO-level services for businesses on an ad hoc or re-occurring basis. The trick as per all of your decisions as a start-up manager is choosing your Virtual CTO carefully. For example, our engineers have represented such firms from 1st to 3rd line to management and CTO level and it is this experience that enables Edge to offer value beyond your Infrastructure. We have sat on your side of the table and we understand your requirements. We will continue to understand those requirements as they evolve in-line with your operation. We only represent firms within this sector so we truly understand and appreciate the demands of the industry.

Whether you have a requirement for an ad hoc project, new system implementation, or simply advice on current industry trends and themes, Edge CTO Advisory can work with you as acting CTO to meet any internal or 3rd party requirement. This can be particularly important when you have to go through investor due diligence. Such advisory services have helped clients undergoing due diligence which eventually led to in-excess of $1 billion in single additional investment tickets. We can provide you with a set of policies and controls based on your current specific level of requirement, and which take account of future needs.

As a start-up manager, you may want to seek an independent CTO to act with your interests at heart in order to further spread your service provider risk. This approach will also assist in validating the credentials of your service provider by ensuring that you have an independent CTO managing that relationship.

As a form of outsourcing the Virtual CTO can allow investment managers to defer capital investments, whether it is purchasing servers or hiring people. The UK regulator the FCA champions the use of service providers but it encourages firms to make sure they manage them as a risk. This plays well into the Virtual CTO concept as many firms recognise that they do not have the skills or experience in-house and look to a Virtual CTO to manage vendor relationships for them. At Edge, we absolutely make recommendations with the client firm's interest at heart, and not those of the service providers. Having an independent CTO can help with validating other business relationships to your board.

Most service providers, ourselves included, offer their own Virtual CTO services. Having a partner and management team at ETG that has represented multi-billion dollar firms at CTO level for many years, makes this one of our core competencies. To go one step further, you could appoint an independent CTO in order to spread your service provider risk whilst gaining a truly independent view at CTO level.

Beyond Infrastructure and growing trends such as cyber security, there are regulatory requirements these days around business continuity, data retention, portfolio management systems, and compliance etc. These are all typical areas where a Virtual CTO can add value. The traditional role of a CTO goes much further than the boundaries of infrastructure and systems provision alone. Aligning IT policies, procedures, budgets, and practise alongside a firm's specific business strategy is also within the remit of a traditional CTO and a good virtual CTO should adopt a similar mentality. Much like everything else in the world of outsourcing, a good virtual CTO should closely replicate the values and functions of a traditional in-house CTO and look to build a very strong relationship with a customer at c-suite and executive level. This relationship is more often than not with the COO of a firm, as many COO's assume much of the responsibility previously taken by a CTO.

**Current Issue – Cybersecurity**

One of the biggest trending themes in recent times is that of Security and more specifically, Cyber Security. Much like "Cloud", "Cyber Security" is another phrase bandied around, but which has implications not well understood. Cyber Secuity captures all of the technological risks in the industry that could pose a threat to an organisation. At Edge, we understand and recognise such risks, and treat it as an evolving threat.

There have been several high profile cases of cyber-attacks in recent years. In support for WikiLeaks, there were orchestrated attacks against Visa, Paypal, and MasterCard. Citi, Google Mail, and Google Docs were hacked by China; Sony Playstation Network lost its entire database; the CIA and US government websites have been attacked; US drones were hacked by Iran. There was the HeartBleed virus, Crypto Locker Outbreak, attacks on Office 365, Outlook.com and of course, the i-cloud photo hacks.

Risks are not always associated with threats from the outside. A start-up manager with on premise IT Infrastructure may also be viewed as a risk to investors. Is the comms room locked? Who has access? Do you employ 24 hour cleaners? Are windows locked? Do you adhere to a clear desk policy? Are workstations locked? The list is endless and can seem like quite a minefield for the start-up manager. At Edge, we encourage firms to appoint an independent 3rd party to conduct a full penetration test. A penetration test is an exercise where a security firm will purposely test your network from beyond your firewall, in addition to testing risks inside your own office. Penetration tests are a good exercise and they will <u>always</u> highlight risks within your environment.

At Edge, we document all annual security tests and collectively review the results from each client whether they have their own on premise IT systems or whether they host with us. This process means that we have in place a security-focused baseline set of controls by design as part of our HFB platform. If you use a Fully Managed Private Cloud Platform  from day 1 you get a lot of these additional security enhancements purely by association, as they are embedded and included in most reputable offerings. This means that by design many of the common risks highlighted by most penetration tests are already accounted for when products such as Edge HFB are implemented. Our focus on security enhancements also extends to service such as Disaster Recovery, Mobile Device Management, Data Loss Prevention, Web Filtering, and Intrusion Detection for all hosted client systems.

Cyber Security is very much a trending theme and is a phrase that is rightly attracting the attention of governing bodies and investors. Our approach at Edge is to simply raise awareness. All of our clients operate within Financial Services and it is now believed that Cyber criminals regard certain financial services companies, particularly the smaller and mid-size ones, as relatively easy targets. A successful breach at one of these smaller organisations could give them access to important information, client funds, strategy info, trading models, or, they could be seen as a conduit to other desirable targets such as banks or larger broker dealers. The cyber defences of such firms are often perceived to be easier to penetrate than those of larger organisations.

Cyber Threats are a very real issue and whilst it is important to raise awareness on this topic in isolation, it is equally important to stress the importance of a strong and correctly implemented IT Security policy. A strong policy that is frequently reviewed on an annual basis will mean that your business is correctly and appropriately prepared for any type of security threat and it should include things such as corporate documentation (data usage policies, IT Security policy, asset register, insurance, Business Continuity Plans etc etc) all of which should be reviewed annually, self-assessments (risk assessments that identify your type of business, areas of operation, and understanding what products are available to mitigate each risk), and of course IT Security Products, where applicable. By association with Edge, you get all of this out of the box as part of our hosted platform with Policy sets, documentation, and controls, handed over immediately after agreements have been signed.

At Edge, our security services are a powerful and comprehensive tool for Hedge Fund managers to gain insight into what is truly happening within their critical systems. From understanding an organisation's vulnerability to supporting organisations who must meet OCIE standards, Edge uses a targeted monitoring system to identify activity within an organisation. Data is continuously gathered, audited, and reported outlining security related changes and activity. We are experts in security design and monitoring, proactive resolution, response and alert via our dedicated 24x7x365 operation centre for any security incident of any scale.

## WHAT MAKES EDGE TECHNOLOGY GROUP DIFFERENT FROM OTHER SERVICE PROVIDERS?

What makes Edge different from other service providers? Well from an Infrastructure perspective, not much. We do not invent technology at Edge. We work and partner with respected and industry established vendors whose systems are seen in financial services firms all over the world. If you look in our Datacenter versus anyone else's Datacenter, you will not find any black magic or black box formula. Client feedback suggests that the value add services we offer goes beyond the simple provision of an IT Infrastructure. Whilst important, it is the expertise behind it that makes a real difference. We are not the cheapest provider in the market today but value goes beyond simple commercial terms. We are not always ideally suited to those that do not share our ethos and principles on day 1 operation. It is the prospective client that recognises that Technology is an investment and not an expense, that we can truly help the most. To launch a successful Hedge Fund, you need to build an IT and operational platform, that can accommodate high availability, redundancy, automation and scale, whilst focussing heavily on the ever changing plethora of governing body and investor trends. We will only build and deliver solutions that meet these main principles and if appetite and/or budgets do not allow us to deliver an

Infrastructure that meets such requirements, we will not be an appropriate partner. Our ethos is to provide a platform that enables a firm to not only launch, but to succeed and evolve in-line with the needs of their business.

## QUESTIONS TO ASK A PROSPECTIVE IT SERVICE PROVIDER

What are the costs of your service, tiered service cost and provision?

What is your client loss experience?

Your own staff turnover?

Designated Key contact person and back-up person?

How many people on the account of a start-up manager?

What is your typical response time?

Have you used your disaster recovery capability yet?

In what way do you help with cyber security?

## FURTHER HELP

One of the benefits of launching a firm in the current market is the number of executive groups available that are on hand to offer advice to those in the industry. A service provider such as ourselves are only ever going to tell you how good we are and we are only ever going to give you references from clients that we know are happy with our service. Whilst we truly believe that we can offer you both a unique and respectable service, we should absolutely still be managed as a risk. In this new age of increased regulation and cyber security, in addition

211

to the advice that you can seek from peers, prime brokers, and governing bodies, there are an ever increasing number of executive groups formed on the basis of providing others in the space, specifically start-ups, with the independent advice required when considering a new venture. Pre engagement, when seeking advice from a service provider who may benefit commercially from any advice for services that is taken, you may question the integrity of such advice.

One of the best groups I have come across in recent times that can offer truly independent advice is The Alternative Investment Technology Executive Club (AITEC) https://www.aitec.org

AITEC is a group of senior hedge fund technology officers that have created a single, all-encompassing DDQ for vendors in what they hope will become an industry standard for due diligence. AITEC has crafted a 'super-set of requests' for service providers to help streamline the due diligence process among managers. An extensive document comprising 14 sections and more than 200 questions was drafted in November of 2014 by AITEC 's internal working group and it covers the full spectrum of service providers. Along with technology firms the DDQ will also include prime brokers, compliance consultants, accounting firms and other trading counterparties. The DDQ asks questions on everything from access controls and network security to incident response policies and vendor software practices. At Edge we have our own Service Provider Risk Assessment and we would encourage any manager of any size to have their chosen service providers complete such DDQ's prior to agreeing terms for services of any kind.

## Closing Advice

We have spoken thus far about the products and services we offer that can assist a start-up manager. There are many additional services beyond those discussed thus far that can assist with other firms and we represent many existing clients with AUM ranging from $1 - $65 billion, and headcounts from 5 – 5000. You will face many different crossroads throughout your journey as a start-up manager as positive performance increases AUM, and healthy AUM attracts varying tiers of investor. Make sure the decisions you make on Day 1 are not made with a view that they will be the right decisions forever.

A service provider might be right for you on day 1 but as you evolve and your operational demand increases, it may be more effective to adopt more of a hybrid model in the years to come. Those trading their own capital whilst adopting a proof-of-concept approach may be happy to work with public cloud platforms on day-1 but after years of positive performance, an investor looking to treble your AUM may cause you to re-think and consider privately managed systems. The key to success is to review your business on an annual basis. Review contracts, review partnerships, and review service providers and treat them all as a risk. Although your contractual obligations to date may have suited you well, such annual reviews will ensure your service providers are meeting the requirements of your current need, and that they have the capacity to meet the requirement of your future needs too.

**CONTACT INFORMATION**

Edge Technology Group

**Primary Contact:** Tom Woollard

EMEA & Asia Managing Director

+44 (0) 20 3535 7810

twoollard@edgetg.co.uk

**Alternative contact:** Jim Nekos, Founding Partner & CEO

+1 203 742 7810

jnekos@edgetg.com

Switchboard: +44 (0}203 535 7800

**Website:** www.edgetg.com

**Address:** 6 Duke Street St James's,
London, SW1Y 6BN

# Chapter 10. Perspective Of An Experienced Hedge Fund COO

By George Alexander of A UK-based Hedge Fund

## About the author

*George Alexander has been involved in running hedge fund businesses since 1999. He has been through three hedge fund start-ups based in London, each with a dominant founder/CIO. He has also been a participant in the institutional money management form of hedge fund management. He has seen growth and stasis in a hedge fund business and has had to deal with all the types of external parties – investors, regulators and service providers.*

*The following are his thoughts on starting out to run a hedge fund management business in 2017.*

## To plan a route you need to know your destination

You absolutely have to know what you are building towards. I had an experience in which we built a business to run $750m of assets based on a research-driven process and executing a long/short European equity strategy. It eventually became a business running $5bn of assets invested globally in a long-biased style. It had a significant managed account for a major investor plus had seeded other managers, all within two years. As a management and ops team we were insufficiently resourced and always playing catch up. If we would have known where we were going we would not have started with only

10 people. The lesson is to have a clear ides of your destination from the off.

(In this previous firm) we gave ourselves more to cope with than we needed to in currencies - we were Euro denominated but most of the investments were in US Dollars and most of the investors were themselves Dollar-based. Logically we should have been a Dollar-denominated Master Fund. It would have made life simpler to have got that structurally right at the beginning.

In the latest start-up in which I am involved, we are not going to have an inception like David Fear's Thunderbird, which started with $1.5bn. We are going to start small with money from people that know and trust us. We are going to have to prove through performance that other investors should take us seriously. That has inferences in terms of cash-flow planning and therefore in our ability to commit to costs (regular and one-off expenses).

One way to reduce costs is to make everyone (each staff member) a partner in the business. However there is a risk in that - the junior staff member, say in operations, might peel off (leave) because they can't afford to live on no salary for any length of time.

The principle is that if you as the owner of the business want to have a lot of control (of the equity and strategic decision making), then setting up the business is going to cost you more because you are going to have to pay for employees. This is also a cultural consideration - if you set up a true partnership then your initial costs are going to be lower.

# GIVEN THE COST AND EFFORT, CONSIDER SHOULD YOU EVEN BOTHER?

If you are a great portfolio manager you are probably being paid a ton of money.

It costs my firm's owner a million Pounds to sit here, and it took 15 months. That is the period between when his decision to go ahead was made and starting to manage money. The period to launch was three months longer than we expected. We used the time to write procedures, and the traders paper-traded to test systems and get mentally ready to invest by staying in tune with markets.

It will probably cost him another million Pounds before costs are exceeded by income.

On top of that he will have to keep 13 weeks of costs in the bank for regulatory purposes.

We are a total of nine people now, and we have been that many since six months before launch. The wage bill is £48,000 a month - so that adds up to a pre-launch cost of nearly £300,000 on its own.

There is cash going out and income forgone, for no guarantee that you are going to succeed. You have to explain to your spouse that there will be no money coming in but there will be money going out in the interregnum between leaving a job and breaking even. And when there is some profitability the income will be low and volatile, in contrast to the costs which are high and not volatile!

On the point of whether it is worthwhile taking up the challenge of setting up a hedge fund management company, here are few numbers to chew over. If you end up running a billion Dollar hedge fund you make $10m in management fees and maybe the same again in performance fees. Say you make $15-20m a year and it cost you $3m in embedded costs to get there. That is a great bet if you are have a substantial net worth already, if you are worth $50m. Taking the entrepreneurial risk with 6% of your net assets with such a potential pay-off is worthwhile,

It would be different for, say a rising star equity manager at a major investment management firm. They may be on a salary plus bonus of $500k-$750k, and not have accumulated much wealth as yet. They may want their name over the door, but the risk/reward is then very different for them.

Other factors to take into account are the extended lead-time to get to launch (including the length of time it now takes to get regulatory approval), and the fact that the costs of being in the business have gone up. The available margins in running a hedge fund management company are significantly lower than they were pre-Credit Crunch. Not the least are the increased costs of compliance, but also property costs in prime locations, human resource costs, and oversight costs (external directors, custodians etcetera) are all higher than they were in the boom times.

As a six or nine person team you will not be surrounded by the same environment as you would get at Fidelity or Blackrock. What would be missing would be the intangible support network of flow, ideas and being surrounded by smart people. For sure, the frequent corporate management contact would not be there for a start-up hedge fund. So, as a start-up manager, you need to know what you need to know to be effective as an investor or trader.

## SYSTEM SELECTION EXPERIENCE

I have not used start-up consultants for the launches I have been involved with. Prime brokers have offered good advice, including explaining what the choices are for systems and service providers. KB

Associates have been extremely helpful in managing the processes in the Irish aspects of the fund launch [see Chapter 2].

Of all the elements, I have found the Portfolio Management System (PMS) provider to be the most difficult to appropriately identify. For most providers, such as the Administrator, Lawyer, Auditors and Accountants it is possible to list strengths and weaknesses for a rational decision. Further those counterparties know what they are doing in regard to working with hedge funds, and have established ways of working. To a degree you have to bend towards them, rather than the other way around, at least for a small start-up.

The purchasing of the PMS, OMS (Order Management System), EMS (Execution Management System) and risk management software and compliance module are all subtle decisions because they impact the front office, and the investment professionals are used to a particular workflow from where they previously worked.

As an example, the CIO of one fund wanted to use a physical trade blotter, rather than automatically-timed-and-generated on-screen tickets. That concept was at least 15 years out-of-date, and was not going to fit with aiming for a paperless office. He was persuaded otherwise. It worked out that the orders of that firm were visible to the whole of the front office in a Bloomberg chat room, so there can be work-arounds in this area.

Readers should be aware that system selection decisions can be a source of some risk to the partners in potentially raising tensions. These system elements are never discarded lightly, so the decisions once made will stand over multiple years.

As the COO I was deeply involved in the process of selecting the PMS - I made sure that many hands were dipped in the blood of that decision. I wanted a broad buy-in to the decision, to minimise subsequent grumbling from the different trader teams. I want to avoid anyone saying "why isn't the PMS showing me the number I want," because even in paper trading that has happened.

A difficulty in selecting and implementing a PMS is that a lot of the things that will eventually be done to customise the system are difficult for a COO to know in advance. The investment team members will know what they want when they see an output from the PMS, but that is after the event. They don't know what questions they are going to be asking of the system - in terms of attribution (the badges and flags of trading), or why the P&L is calculated the way it is. If we knew exactly how a system is going to be used we could specify exactly the right PMS at the beginning. But we don't and can't know. That gap can be big.

In a demo room with a large screen, a system being sold looks easy to use in the hands of product experts. Get it installed and a few months on in time, and finding that entry screen or output report yourself is a different proposition given the enormous complexity - breadth and depth - of modern systems, I would say from experience.

When it came to OMSs we looked at cheap systems that were limited, and more integrated and higher-priced systems. We went with the more expensive system because it will be better value over the medium-to-long term despite the upfront cost. It is also intuitive to look at and use. Fair play to our CEO/CIO in that he understood that it was better value if we were serious about our future growth. It has a collateral benefit too: when potential investors come to do their due diligence it signals that we were anxious to build for quality to begin with.

We chose from a long list of ten different system suppliers. The long list was whittled down to five with whom we did the full assessment process, and then chose between the two best as we saw it. We were able to line up the last two on a directly comparable basis, though one of the two outsourced risk measurement to another company (users can have a direct relationship with that supplier or pay and receive via the principal system supplier).

It turned out that we bought every component from the same supplier rather than ending up with a mosaic of different components from a variety of firms. That has some advantages in integration, and maybe cost. Each of the ten providers all started their business in different areas of system offering (OMS or risk management or PMS - which is the firm's DNA) then all became suppliers on a broader, more holistic, basis. If you like, each starting from a different place and ending up at the same one.

## SERVICE PROVIDER EXPERIENCE

Our firm is using a synthetic prime brokerage capability rather than a full-blown prime brokerage outfit. That meant that the full hedge fund consulting and capital introduction (cap intro) services have not been available to me. We have had to do it all ourselves in terms of long lists and short lists and meeting and assessing potential service providers, including systems providers. I didn't do a search as such – the providers more or less all came to me.

Registration is an issue for costs of running a fund. We have an Irish UCITS Fund, but have spent a lot of money on registrations beyond Eire. To pro-actively market (not relying on reverse solicitation) I have to have a paying agents and a fund representative (office) in each EU country I want to sell into. It costs €2,500 per country. In my view paying agents take the money off you but don't do much for it. They nominally assist Fund Administrators in the paying and receiving of subscriptions, and make your Prospectus available to investors (on your own website!).

We appointed a custodian/depository (a Trustee for the Fund, based in Ireland) after looking at two potential providers. I looked at a comparison of every conceivable cost for the service for the two of them, but chose on that basis that the sales contact for one of them was particularly attentive and good at getting back to us. It has turned out that we have not seen or heard of that particular person since he finished selling to us, but I suppose he has done his job for his employers!

You have to come up with a fund structure that investors will want to buy. For the clients you have lined up, or will be targeting, that may be an AIF or UCITS. Whichever you choose, it has to be appropriate for your intended client base.

I have heard of a fund that was set up with a structure to suit the CIO. The CIO's new fund was set up as a sub-fund of someone else's Cayman Islands fund. He thought the structure would be quicker in time-to-market and ultimately cheaper to operate than ones commonly seen for hedge funds. He may have been right by those two criteria, but the novelty of the structural arrangement completely turned off potential investors. All the meetings with potential clients were dominated by the legal structure. He had to change to a more conventional fund structure to get any serious investor to commit capital, thus making the whole thing no quicker to get to launch and ultimately more expensive for him/the Fund.

+In this particular case the CIO owned the whole venture and it took 30%-plus of his net worth to set up the management company and fund. As a consequence I heard that he made many decisions to make the costs as cheap as possible. Investors pick up on that and it does not play well with them.

# MARKETING

We have one marketing executive, and it is a big world to market to, so we are about to use a third-party marketer to help us. They may have a modest retainer, but that aside it only costs us if we raise capital, and it adds bandwidth to our capital raising effort. We think using a 3PM should increase the probability of us reaching out capital milestones. This is partly because the external marketers effectively prise open the door for their hedge fund clients by working their own networks, but also because all 3PMs have to do their own due diligence. To the extent that the 3PM is rated by investors in hedge funds, the funds the 3PM chooses to work with are accredited a hygiene factor, and maybe some credibility.

At the same time we are keen that utilising a 3PM does not act as a substitute for a marketing strategy. Our CIO in his previous role had employed what many people would consider a full marketing team in advance of raising a lot of capital. So he probably has a more constructive take on marketing expense than most new hedge fund CIOs. Maybe that is why he sanctioned the spending on a dedicated hedge fund CRM (Client Relationship Management system), which again reflects taking marketing and client servicing seriously. The cost of a hedge fund CRM is upwards of $5,000 per user per year. A good CRM should allow you to weigh your best prospects appropriately and help you target your resources.

We have also engaged a lead-generator company. The way they operate is to contact investors by phone and ask them what strategies they are currently interested in. They have given us two leads a week. We reckon the cost of that service is about a third of the cost of hiring a senior marketer for a year, and you don't have the ongoing commitment.

The marketing strategy should be aligned with the fund structure. So there is a marketing implication in having a UCITS structure or a single country designation like the French QIF. We have a UCITS structure ourselves, but are looking to add a Delaware feeder to it. That is because we have targeted some US investors that one of our staff has connections with.

My final investor-related point is on fund terms. A new investment management company represents a higher risk to an investor than an established one. So it is appropriate to reflect that higher risk for investors in lower initial fees. In our case our first wave of investors paid 1/2 % management fee. The next wave of investors paid 3/4 % management fee, and later investors will pay 1 1/4%. Also smaller funds have a higher TER and this fee scale offsets that.

As a new hedge fund manager you need to know how to reflect your investment process to investors. You have to give potential investors a story – tell them that you see the world in a slightly different way from their existing managers. That will add credibility to telling them that you aim to deliver a different return stream for them. The investment process has to be interesting in the telling and repeatable. You have to be able to articulate your process.

It is important for the principal of a new hedge fund management company to move from being a fund manager to being a CEO. Being the owner of a business is different from being a portfolio manager. There is nowhere else to look but yourself to oversee a whole bunch of responsibilities – compliance, disaster recovery and hiring, for example. The new manager should surround themselves with trusted colleagues who can make good their own deficiencies. In the end the best businesses work for all the stakeholders involved.

# CHAPTER 11. NEW MANAGERS FROM AN INVESTOR'S PERSPECTIVE

## A Q&A with Global Asset Management's Anthony Lawler

*"Hedge Fund Insight" Publisher Simon Kerr talked to Anthony Lawler about what new managers need to be aware of when it comes to meeting their potential investors or seeders.*

## About the interviewee

*Anthony Lawler is Head of Portfolio Management, GAM Alternative Investments Solutions (AIS). In this role he sits on the firm's AIS Investment Committee, and he leads portfolio investment decision making for all Alternative Investments Solutions portfolios. He also has a GAM Group strategy role to source potential new investment managers to join GAM.*

## About Global Asset Management

GAM is a global asset management firm in which the core investment business is complemented by private labelling solutions, which include management company and other support services for third-party asset managers. The Group employs around 1,000 people in 11 countries with investment centres in London, Cambridge, Zurich, Hong Kong, New York, Milan and Lugano. The investment managers are supported by an extensive global distribution network. The Group sells to a wide range of client segments such as institutions, wholesale intermediaries, financial advisers, and private investors. GAM has a long history of investing in hedge funds and has repeatedly backed emerging manager talent at an early stage.

**(Simon Kerr) What are business conditions like for new managers starting out now?**

(Anthony Lawler) The environment for start-up managers has changed completely since the credit crunch and it is much tougher for them to start out now. In addition to the growing cost of regulation, monitoring and compliance, it is much harder for prime brokers to justify the costs incurred with smaller hedge funds, so some start-up funds battle to even find a prime broker. More generally, prime brokers don't want to take as much risk or offer as much leverage as they used to. Equity managers specifically have come under more pressure – equity securities have a higher capital charge on the bank's balance sheet compared with prime broking on futures or currencies.

In sum it has become materially more difficult to be a new or emerging manager both due to the higher costs incurred and the challenge of finding service providers.

**Do you have any hard-and-fast rules on the number of people in a new hedge fund management company?**

We have no hard rules on the number of people that need to be involved in a newly formed hedge fund management company. Where you have day one capital of $100m, a fund manager with a ten-year track record, but only one person to do sales, marketing operations and compliance, then it is likely we wouldn't invest. We know that in those circumstances the lead portfolio manager is going to have to spend too much of her or his time addressing non-investment issues. That is too much of a distraction and the investment returns could suffer.

There is no magic number for support staff, but the closer that number is to one the more difficult it is to say that the investment side will not be impacted by the non-investment side.

This is related to another development. We think that it has become increasingly difficult to have an (investment) edge as a hedge fund manager. The immediacy and abundance of information, and the cheapness of analytical engines to handle vast volumes of data mean that it is much more difficult to exploit the kind of edge that managers had in the 1980's and '90's, and even into the Noughties.

It is now more expensive to run a hedge fund: you need more people in the back office than you did in the past. Otherwise it is likely your front office person, who is already operating in an environment where it is more difficult to create alpha, will be distracted because they have to help on the operations side. In this scenario you must expect your average outcome to be worse than historical outcomes in performance terms.

The only reason to back a manager early is if the investor thinks they are better than other managers (in expected performance terms) and that the business side of the firm will be well managed. This has become a tougher call to make on both points. We do not seek out small managers, but rather we are size and business-stage agnostic. We are looking for managers with real edge, regardless of whether they are a new launch or not. All of that said, we find that given our depth of research, we do have more tolerance of the risks associated with investing in an early stage manager than most.

For the portfolio manager considering setting up a fund, it is critical that the main investment person understands the cost and complexity and distraction potential of operating a hedge fund business in this current environment. The world has changed. Gone are the days when a portfolio manager could set up a fund with one non-investment person and a few tens of millions of dollars.

**At what stage do you meet a new manager?**

We will meet a manager or trader before they have even left their current shop as we can offer advice on how to structure their offering, for example on liquidity terms or cutting out certain exposures that add complexity without enough value. For example we have an arrangement with a global macro firm where only the trades from the two portfolio managers we like are in the managed account. We don't take exposure to the rest of the team.

We typically don't do a detailed, documented investment assessment until after regulatory registration and both back office and front office processes have been established. Part of our judgement is based on the CFO or COO, so they have to be in place. We meet those people, and establish their calibre, before we consider investing in the fund.

**How do you think about the significance of the COO or CEO, compared to the CIO?**

We look at the roles completely differently. We might score the Chief Investment Officer) on a scale, say, out of ten. The CIO may be a 9/10 compared to others in his strategy at, say, 7-8/10. So on the investment side we are looking for relative strength. But we see the COO (or CEO if the CIO has not taken the CEO title) as needing to reach a threshold – so it is binary and often an absolute level that must be obtained. He might be a 7 which we would accept and monitor, but he can't be a 5. A 5/10 would mean we would not invest given the risk that the COO is not as experienced as we require.

One thing that has become increasingly important is regulatory risk. If a manager doesn't do things correctly there can be an issue with the regulators. As a result, the COO or CEO having experience with the regulators and their way of operating is very important today. Our operational due diligence burden has grown because we need to be able to evaluate a manager's understanding of regulatory issues on top of all other operational risks.

There are firms out there that help start-up managers negotiate the path with regulators, but we don't insist they are used. They comfort us in that managers then understand the magnitude of the challenges involved. If a consultant is used, the managers are much less likely to build operational and compliance processes that are analogous to a square table with three legs. A well-intentioned manager with an investment edge may build an operation that is equivalent to a three-legged table - someone will lean on the un-legged corner and the whole operation can fall down. Having professionals involved materially lowers the risk of that happening.

**What else do you look for in new managers?**

All managers have blind spots - we want to know what they are. We have to know what risks we are taking when we get involved.

We ask lots of questions on investing, people and the business. We do have a detailed assessment form, but we don't use that in our early stage meetings. Rather we let the conversation flow and explore how the manager thinks. Then, after the meeting, we put notes in a framework that we have for the purpose. We don't have either a tick box mentality.

Although we are size agnostic, we do want a manager to be large enough to pay his team and to keep the lights on. We tend not to invest in managers that will have less than $100m in assets under management in their launch quarter and typically we look for this number to be far higher, say $300m. We look at the level of working capital in the fund management company. Through our process we knock out people where there is risk that they can't pay the full operating costs (excluding investment staff salaries). Indeed, we see those risks for anyone running under $300m now, such is the unavoidable cost of being in the business.

## And at what stage are you prepared to meet a new hedge fund manager?

We will meet informally at any stage. A first meeting for a manager that is still working at their prior shop, say a large hedge fund group, may be over a cup of coffee. Then we work to triangulate to a view on the skill of the prospective manager. In our assessment we put a lot of weight on the views of people who have worked closely with the nascent manager. We have, for example, off-the-record conversations with the trader or analyst that sat next to the prospective manager. We do that kind of screening early as you can appreciate this is a difficult selection process through which most managers fail to meet our criteria.

Even coming from a big hedge fund, similar to coming off a prop desk, you don't necessarily know why that person made money. This is different to simply accepting the prospective manager's view on how and why he/she makes money. The person sitting next to them for the past decade will have a view on whether they were just acting on information only available in the context of the firm or whether the investment professional added significant value themselves outside of flow. The first meeting often involves us trying to encourage the manager to deviate from their prepared presentation. In fact we don't even want to see the presentation in the meeting. We like the manager to just talk about why they think they could have an edge in reasonably efficient markets.

I used to pound into my research staff working in funds-of-funds that any time you ask about the contents of the manager's presentation you are going to get a prepared answer. So rather than ask about a top 5 position, ask about the 11th ranked position, or about a newer position rather than a full sized one. Zoning in on that position we ask questions like "why is it this size, how come you haven't changed its' size, why isn't it your largest position?" not to refute their investment thesis, but to understand how they came to their thesis.

**You have mentioned the word "edge" a few times could you expand on the concept?**

We have a good record of determining whether a manager is better than their peer group. But even if they are, are they *really* good enough or just a bit better than average? Do they have an edge that is big enough and sustainable, or are they just intelligent people? We need to find enough managers that add value so that when we get the inevitable underperformers (within a portfolio of funds) there are managers adding value to make up the shortfall.

It is much more difficult to have an information edge now - it used to be that managers could get this a few times a year, but today you can, for example, get timely information on Azerbaijan on Bloomberg. Information is far more instantly available so information edge is harder to come by.

We have looked quite a bit at managers trying to extract useful information from Big Data. We have spent more than two years looking at Big Data and machine-learning. There is a massive amount of information that market participants use to make decisions in markets but we have yet to find a silver bullet that consistently reduces data mass down to consistent trading signals. Where we are seeing some added value is in the use of data smaller and specialist data (and not really Big Data) where the insight is drawn out systematically and where the manager is able to act on that insight quickly.

The edge in a manager often comes down to how they interpret information and then how they manage risk. Given the instantaneous data available, today it is more about how the trader interprets the importance of that information, rather than the information itself that determines their edge. Then portfolio management and risk management are significant edge determinants for many investing styles. Does the manager tend to protect capital in tough periods and then get outsized returns when a thesis plays out as expected? Those characteristics over time add a lot of compounded return and edge.

## Are there any investment strategies you avoid?

We tend not to invest in strategies focused on small and illiquid markets. We steer clear of anything that might indicate that the manager could impact the market or have market control. Say in emerging markets for example, where despite having the potential to invest in many underlying emerging markets, they concentrate on just one country. That is a flag for us and requires close inspection – we would sooner avoid those kinds of situations.

We don't invest in managers who bet on longevity risk. It is a legitimate investment strategy, but it doesn't fit with what we do.

Generally speaking we don't like complexity; we don't like very structured trades, or esoteric positions. We avoid overly-geared and/or overly-structured strategies like CDO-squared, or anything with lots of layers to it.

We tend not to invest in very-leveraged multi-strategy funds. When a liquidity problem arises in markets or there is generalised de-leveraging these funds can come under funding pressure given their leverage. In these sorts of highly geared multi-strategy funds as an investor you often don't really know what risks you own - despite the transparency reports, we may not be sure what risks we are exposed to. So we tend to avoid the problem all together by not allocating to this style of fund.

We generally do not have a problem with mortgage-backed or asset backed strategies. If they are run in a unleveraged or lowly-levered manner, these strategies have definable risks similar to those in high yield and investment grade credit investing. We invest in direct lending strategies and peer-to-peer lending. We can cope with illiquid strategies as long as our clients have that same illiquidity tolerance. For example the manager we most recently incorporated into GAM runs a real estate lending strategy. They run vehicles with a roughly 7 year investment horizon. So we can accept some illiquidity in the right circumstances - where it is integral to the underlying investments.

**How scalable must the investment strategy be?**

We would rather a manager that we get involved with early be capable of running at least $1-2bn in total.

If the manager does not have that capacity then we might not reach our target allocation size and thus it be a poor use of our research resources.

**Does a new manager have to have an audited track record?**

The best track record is an audited track record where the manager was the main decision-maker. It is better if the track record is three years or longer, and each additional year of track record helps. It is helpful if the manager has been through a full cycle or more for their strategy or cycle of the markets. But even when there is a track record, it is important to try to understand the positions and decisions that led to the track record. For example, in assessing a manager's experience of 2008 you have to understand the exposures the managers had going into the crisis and the reasons behind them. Some managers had low exposure by chance, and so we have to understand the individual circumstances. If there is no audited track record then an unaudited track record from a Separately Managed Account (SMA) or book is the next best form of track record. The third best form of track record is a carve-out (from a fund with multiple portfolio managers or analysts) including every single trade that that person put on and in the size they made it.

Every other track record is less preferable to the other three mentioned above. A track record from a multi-strategy fund where the size of capital varied over time has the same fallibilities as a prop-desk track record. You tend to never see a bad track record from a prop desk-style variable capital allocation regime. To take account of that we will talk through with a manager what the maximum and minimum amounts of capital that were allocated to them in each year. Then one can take the absolute dollar profit and work out what an approximation of the returns were. Very often in those circumstances the capital put to work can be too low and too variable. The track record has to reflect that no returns would have been generated when the opportunity set was poor and they didn't have any trades on.

### Any advice for someone starting out on this path?

A critical piece of advice for those starting out is to not exaggerate your past. Investors will do their due diligence and speak to others in the industry and won't rely just on those that you gather round the meeting room table.

Some will be cut from the prospective fund list because they have exaggerated their role or money-making abilities in the past.

When it comes to other advice, I would say be cautious in signing up with a seeding partner or accelerator. I would suggest that you only sign up with someone if they are giving you value, which in crude monetary terms is $100m or more in assets and a multi-year capital lock-up, or they pay full fees. That arrangement will get you off the ground.

I'd suggest that you don't start at all if you are not going to open with $100m or have commitments to be at $100m really quickly. Figure out how you are going to stay in business for three years. You need working capital for that long because it can be a slow start raising capital.

## How can investors help hedge fund managers setting up apart from capital?

Seasoned investors can help you with the design of the product. Investors have a clear idea of what will work commercially. So they can help with the parameters of the balance sheet – the level of volatility that investors prefer, how big your shorts should be relative to your longs, that kind of thing. The fund manager might otherwise have decided on a structure or a level of risk taking that won't appeal to potential buyers.

Sometimes investors that put hedge fund managers into business will effect introductions to other sources of capital. So a family office will know other family offices, and an institutionally-focused fund of funds will know pension plans and endowments.

It is very helpful to have your story in good shape in your pitch book. It should be straightforward, professional and look good.

## What questions will you ask a manager looking to set up?

This is by no means an exhaustive list, but the type of things we ask are:

What is your investment style?

What is your investment philosophy for engaging with markets?

Can you outline what makes your strategy and returns repeatable in future?

How do you make excess returns? Why does the market not arbitrage that away?

What kind of team have you had around you?

How will you replicate that environment?

Walk through your historical performance attribution.

Walk through trade structuring and how you adjust positions as pricing changes.

## What are the terms of business like now?

Fees of 2-and-20 at the launch of a fund now are very rare. It is quite common these days to have something like a founders' class of shares. That class of shares may be open for the first year of trading. If you are involved at an early stage you can get 1-and-15, and pushing for it, sometimes even 1-and-10.

We don't ourselves typically commit capital for two or three years, but other early stage investors do do that. We are pleased to see that because it gives stability to the management company and the owners can plan on the back of it. It may also give a better chance for the CIO to concentrate on investing. The very best fee breaks can be associated with capital committed over two or three years.

There are typically break clauses, like in an ISDA Agreement, for a drawdown or NAV change. If a normal move is 10% for the investment strategy the break clause could be for a 30% fall. So the risk to the manager is that in a 3-standard deviation NAV loss you can lose your locked up capital. The clause which locked in capital would no longer apply.

There may be hurdles in the performance fees. For example the fees could be 1-and-15% with a hurdle of LIBOR plus 5% on the performance fee.

A lot of people are offering monthly liquidity in strategies and firms that would not have offered that in the past. That is partly because of UCITS. So there are funds (in offshore form) that stick to the monthly cycle of reporting and disclosure, but you can see daily NAVs now in onshore versions of hedge fund strategies. Managers have to have in-house systems that can cope with that if they see those more liquid forms as likely sources of capital.

### Does "Most Favoured Nation" Status still apply in providing early stage capital?

The way they work now is that the manager of an emerging fund will give an investor an agreement that no investor of their size who comes in after them will get better terms than they do. Someone who is larger may get a lower annual management fee, but if they are smaller they are unlikely to get that. Some managers have been successful in charging later investors higher fees than the founders share class fees even when the later investors come in larger size.

### Any other advice for a start-up manager?

Managers would be well served to think about which region they are going to raise money from. Each jurisdiction that you are going to raise money from will cost you money up front, with AIFMD in Europe for example. So managers have to think about which countries they are going to raise capital from, whether in the EU, beyond the EU, in Switzerland, and separately the United States. Europe is a big deal to think through – you can't just "do a roadshow" through Europe as you used to be able to.

Managers should not over-estimate their ability to penetrate the U.S. for raising assets. You may think "I only need 1% share of funds raised in a year to succeed in that market." But it is very difficult for a start-up manager to get traction there. If the manager has an audited three-year track record that can be referenced, then it would be good to look for backing from as many seeders/early stage backers as possible in order to get launched. Once they secure some launch capital, being able to immediately market with a three year track record increases the likelihood of securing direct institutional investors.

**Thanks for sharing your knowledge on start-up hedge fund managers Anthony.**

# CHAPTER 12. BACKERS OF EARLY-STAGE HEDGE FUNDS

Just about all investors in hedge funds say that in very particular circumstances they are prepared to be either day-one investors in hedge funds or early stage backers. This chapter lists those that have been active backers of such hedge funds in the last 3-4 years.

Many of the entities listed are based in the United States, though some of those American organizations have a European office. It is harder to get backing from an American source of capital for a European-based manager than a U.S. based manager, but it does happen. A good proposition will surmount the difficulties.

Sources of day-one capital will have their own criteria and processes. Neophyte managers should work with those criteria and processes having done their research on the backers.

Many of the following entries of hedge fund backers come from the list published by industry newsletter "Hedge Fund Alert". Their work is reproduced with permission.

SPONSOR

HQ    *TYPES of FIRMS TARGETED*

CONTACT(S)

COMMENT

## Aurora Investment

Chicago        *Start-up, Emerging*

Justin Sheperd

312-762-6700, jsheperd@aurorallc.com,

Scott Schweeighauser

sschweeighauser@aurorallc.com

Long-established fund-of-funds manager entered seeding business in 2014, when it agreed to back equity-fund shops Adi Capital and Brenham Capital. Later that year, it seeded Sentinel Dome Partners. Invests $50 million to $150 million per manager, in exchange for a share of revenue. Aurora, which runs $7.7 billion overall, for now is funding the initiative with capital from its multi-manager vehicles.

## Bainbridge Partners

London        *Start-up*

Omar Hassan

44-207-590-1804, omar@bainbridgepartners.com

Fund-of-funds manager has yet to hold first close for debut seeding vehicle it began marketing in early 2014. But it can make one-off seed investments using partner and investor capital. In 2015, backed $20 million launch of Alcazar Investment, led by electricity trader Joaquin Narro. Favors Start-ups with at least a couple of hundred million dollars of capacity trading niche strategies in liquid markets.

## Blackstone

New York     *Start-up, Established*

Logan Pritchard

212-390-2757, logan.pritchard@blackstone.com

World's biggest hedge fund investor and most prolific seeder has fully deployed $2.4 billion from second seeding vehicle, the 2010-vintage Blackstone Strategic Alliance Fund 2. Portfolio of 14 Start-ups includes two that have shut down. As of mid-2015, returns were hovering in the low single digits, but were expected to rise. Meanwhile, third seed-capital fund is about halfway toward $1.5 billion equity-raising goal. Separately, Blackstone has finished raising $3.3 billion for a fund that targets minority stakes in mature hedge fund operations. Initial positions include stakes in Magnetar Capital, Senator Investment and Solus Alternative Asset Management.

## Brummer & Partners

Stockholm/London     *Start-up, Emerging, Established*

Klaus Jantti, CEO,

46-8-566-214-80, klaus.jantti@brummer.se

Brummer & Partners is one of Europe's oldest and largest hedge fund management groups with $15bn in AUM. Brummer Multi-Strategy invests in affiliated funds and takes ownership stakes (typically 40%) in partner firms. It backed Benros with $300m, and has cut deals with Canosa in 2013 and Florin Court Capital, Talarium Capital and Arete Capital Partners in 2016. Brummer put $400m into MNJ Capital's Absolute Return Fund in Oct 2014 and redeemed in Feb 2016, a similar time-frame to previous Asian market adventure Orvent Asset Management (2010-12).

## Context Capital

Bala Cynwyd, Pa.    *Start-up, Emerging*

Ron Biscardi

610-538-6100, ron@contextcp.com

Inked first two seed deals in 2012, using partner money to launch Context BH Partners and Green Owl Capital. Hasn't backed a hedge fund launch since, having shifted its focus to managers of alternative mutual funds. But will continue looking at Start-up fund shops on an opportunistic basis. Also runs a hedge fund-conference business it took over from AlphaMetrix following that firm's collapse in 2013.

## Goldman Sachs

New York    *Start-up*

Ryan Roderick

212-902-1000, ryan.roderick@gs.com

Runs a $650 million seed-capital fund that is fully invested and returning about 9% annually. It's unclear if Goldman intends to raise a follow-on seeding vehicle, but it continues to look at seed deals on an opportunistic basis. The seeding business is overseen by Ryan Roderick.


## GCM Grosvenor

Chicago    *Start-up, Emerging*

Jonathan Levin

312-506-6647, jlevin@gcmlp.com,

Michael Kirchner

mkirchner@gcmlp.com

Fund-of-funds giant runs the Spectrum Program, a $475 million seeding vehicle that launched in 2013. Deployed $50 million to $100 million per manager. Last two deals were with Hollis Park Partners (RMBS) and Pinyon Asset Management (Event Driven). Continues to scout fresh prospects, but unclear whether Grosvenor plans to launch a new seed-capital fund or offer deals to clients on a one-off basis.

## Harvest Funds Management

Marblehead, MA.    *Start-up, Emerging*

Eli Kent, Co-Founder and Managing Partner,

781-639-7054, eli@harvestfund.com;

William B. Moody, Co-Founder and Managing Partner,

HFM specializes in structuring investments and ownership interests in promising, newly independent hedge firms.

## Horton Point

New York    *Start-up, Emerging*

Dimitri Sogoloff

212-939-7300, das@hortonpoint.com

After raising an undisclosed amount of capital in 2013, began seeding systematic traders with $1 million to $5 million apiece. Recently expanded acceleration-capital program with an eye toward supporting unaffiliated managers. Runs a managed-account business offering access to some 40 emerging managers, including those backed by Horton Point.

**HS Group**

Hong Kong    *Start-up, Emerging*

Michael Garrow

852-3968-5056, garrow@hsgfunds.com

Founded in 2013 by one-time Blackstone executive Michael Garrow and former Goldman Sachs executive Johannes Kaps to invest in new and emerging hedge fund managers, mostly in Asia. Received Start-up capital and other forms of support from TPG and Gottex Fund Management, which own minority stakes in the business. Backed Zaaba Capital, a Hong Kong shop that launched in late-2015 with $250 million or more. Also backed Pleiad Investment and Zentific Investment, which both launched in 2014.

**IMQubator**

Amsterdam    *Start-up, Emerging*

Jeroen Tielman

31-62-937-9265, information@imqubator.com

Seed-capital fund backed by Dutch pension giant APG hasn't done a deal since 2013. Vehicle nearing the end of its seven-year term, but IMQubator has been trying to raise fresh capital to pursue new deals.

**Infusion Global Partners**

Boston    *Emerging*

John Sinclair

617-869-5945, john.sinclair@infusionglobal.com

Has raised $10 million so far for debut acceleration-capital vehicle. Invests small amounts with each manager in exchange for a cut of profits above a benchmark. Has completed seven deals so far.

## Investcorp

New York    *Start-up, Emerging*

Nick Vamvakas

917-332-5700, nvamvakas@investcorp.com

Seasoned seed investor deploys balance-sheet capital, but is open to working with co-investors. Has vetted more than 2,000 new and emerging managers. Most recently invested an unknown amount of acceleration capital with London-based Eyck Capital. Other deals include a $50 million seed investment in Kingsguard Advisors and a $50 million acceleration-capital investment in Kortright Capital. Also backed Prosiris Capital.

## James Alpha Management

New York    *Start-up, Emerging*

Kevin Greene

212-201-5520, kgreene@jamesalpha.com

Raises capital on deal-by-deal basis to invest alongside partner money. Targets both Start-ups and more-established firms. Completed first seed deal in 2011, when it helped launch a real estate-focused vehicle run by Andrew Duffy. Has backed a handful of other managers including Invicta Capital, which shut down in 2015 due to poor performance.

**Larch Lane Advisors**

Rye Brook, N.Y.     *Start-up, Emerging*

David Katz

914-798-7600, davidkatz@larchlane.com

Mark Jurish, CEO

Manages three hedge fund-seeding vehicles including the $400 million joint-venture seeding fund it launched with PineBridge Investments in 2008, and has $500m in assets in total. Larch Lane is among the most experienced seed investors, having entered the market in 2001. Last known deal, via the PineBridge joint venture, was with C12 Capital in 2011. Larch Lane was taken over by Fiera Capital in 2016.

**Leucadia National**

New York     *Start-up, Emerging*

Nicholas Daraviras

212-284-1700, ndaraviras@leucadia.com

After buying Jefferies in 2013, diversified holding company formed asset-management division that seeks to acquire stakes in new and emerging alternative-investment businesses including hedge fund managers and commodity-trading advisors. In 2014, reached deal with former SAC Capital executive Sol Kumin to seed his Folger Hill Asset Management with $400 million, on condition that it raised at least that amount from other investors. Folger Hill launched in 2015 with $1 billion. Leucadia also owns Topwater Capital, which offers "first loss" seed capital to Start-up fund shops.

## Linear Investments Limited

London        *Start-up, Emerging*

Jerry Lees, chairman

44-203-603-9801, jlees@linearinvestment.com

Helps put small hedge funds into business including bringing in capital providers. A platform for new funds with low cost structuring available. Has a joint venture with Bainbridge Partners called the B&L Seeder Fund.

## Mariner Investment

Harrison, N.Y.        *Start-up, Emerging*

Brendan Minogue

212-880-9247, bminogue@marinercapital.com

Struck deal with Alaska Permanent Fund in 2012 under which it is deploying $500 million to back a dozen new managers, with the idea of incubating them and spinning off the most successful ones. As of September 2014, had backed six managers. Invested other client capital in Robert Heine's Morven Advisors, which launched in 2013. Also has done a number of acceleration deals, and has long backed spinoffs by its own portfolio managers, including Caspian Capital, Pembrook Capital and Tricadia Capital.

## Maverick Capital

Dallas          *Start-up, Emerging*

Bates Brown

212-418-6958, bates.brown@maverickcap.com

Set aside $100 million of proprietary capital in 2011 for its first seeding vehicle. Invests perhaps $20 million per deal, either for a minority ownership stake or cut of revenue. Most recently backed Cloverdale Capital and Westray Capital. Earlier deals were with Sentinel Rock Partners, Sycamore Lane Partners, Totem Point Management and Rinehart Capital, which wound down in 2014 after suffering losses. Still has dry powder. Maverick plans to raise a commingled seeding fund once it has a track record to show. Bates Brown, who oversees the firm's fund-of-funds unit, also runs the seeding business.

## Meritage Group

San Francisco          *Start-up*

Meredith Barth

212-906-8660, mer-hfs@meritagegroup.com

Led by **Nat Simons**, son of Renaissance Technologies founder James Simons, $8 billion firm mainly invests in other managers' hedge funds on behalf of Renaissance partners. Has inked at least five seed deals in recent years, most recently Atalan Partners, led by former Soroban Capital executive David Thomas. Others are Anandar Capital, Hutchin Hill Capital, Lamond Capital and Sarissa Capital. Can write checks of $150 million or more.

## Moody Aldrich Partners

Marblehead, MA       *Start-up, Emerging, Established*

Eli Kent

781-639-7054, eli@harvestfund.com

Finished raising north of $100 million for its debut seeding and acceleration vehicle in 2014 via subsidiary Harvest Funds Management. That capital is now fully deployed, and firm is making additional investments on a deal-by-deal basis, typically $30 million to $50 million per deal. Has backed five firms including Genesis Capital, which former Millennium Management executive Robert DeFranco launched in 2015. Is now looking to take minority equity stakes in more-established firms running up to $1 billion.

## NewAlpha Asset Management

Paris            *Start-up, Emerging, Established*

Antoine Rolland

33-1-44-56-52-34, arolland@newalpha.net

Rozenn Peres, Director

Fabien Dersy, Director of Research

The seeding partnership is signed for a fixed period, on average 8 years, including a 3-year incubation period during which NewAlpha will support the managers in their development, while providing consulting and investment monitoring services for the seeding investors. Backed quant fund Prime Capital this year. Will investment in small, established firms both in the U.S. and Europe as well as Start-ups. Completed three deals in the U.S. in 2014 and 2015: Quest Global Advisors, Sabal Capital and Steamboat Capital. Unit of OFI Asset Management has $700 million of assets in firms running a combined $8 billion.

## Northill Capital

London           *Start-up, Emerging, Established*

Ryan Sinnott

44-207-016-4119, ryan.sinnott@northhill.com

Founded in 2010 by former BNY Mellon executive Jonathan Little with backing from Italy's Bertarelli family. Takes majority stakes in Start-ups as well as established managers looking to cash out partners. In January 2016, bought 60% equity interest in Capital Four, a Copenhagen-based debt manager with €6 billion ($6.5 billion) of assets. Other investments include Goldbridge Capital, ILS specialist Securis Investment Partners and Wellfield Partners. Converted 51% stake in hedge fund backer Alpha Strategic to full ownership in 2013.

## Old Mutual Wealth

London        *Start-up, Emerging*

Paul Craig

44-207-332-7500 paul.craig@omglobalinvestors.com

Old Mutual Wealth's multi-manager unit was a day one investor in the event-driven manager Mygale in the UCITS format early in 2016.

## Paloma Partners

Greenwich, Conn.   *Start-up*

Michael Liebowitz

203-861-3230, mliebowitz@paloma.com

Founded by Donald Sussman in 1989, $3.1 billion firm backs managers representing a range of strategies, but favors quantitative traders.

Seedlings typically run money exclusively for Paloma for some years before raising outside capital. Usually invests $100 million to $150 million per deal, but staked Reef Road Capital with $300 million in 2013. Backed statistical-arbitrage shop AlphaCrest Capital in mid-2014 and Dasoma Capital and Qtrade in 2015.

## Pine Street Alternative Asset Management

New York     *Start-up, Emerging*

Caroline Lovelace

646-415-7200, newmanagers@pinestreetalt.com

Founded in 2011, firm is investing via a $200 million commitment it landed from New York Common Fund in early 2014. Invests seed and acceleration capital in exchange for revenue shares. Focuses in part on women- and minority-owned hedge fund managers. Pine Street is led by former Investcorp executive Lofton Holder.


## Prime Allocation Group

Stamford, Conn.     *Start-up, Emerging*

Andrew Gitlin

203-517-8740, info@primeallocation.com

Began soliciting contributions for debut seed-capital fund in 2015, while scouting prospective deals mainly in Europe and the Middle East.

Targeting Start-ups or emerging managers with less than $150 million of assets. In addition to capital, will offer operational support, including compliance services via partnership with London consultant Lawson Connor. Led by Andrew Gitlin, whose resume includes nine years as chief executive of AIG's alternative-investment division.

## Protege Partners

New York      *Start-up*

Mike Barron

212-784-6321, mb@protegepartners.com

Jeffrey Tarrant, CEO

Makes seed investments of $50 million to $100 million in exchange for cuts of managers' revenues. Runs $2.1 billion via multi-manager funds and separate accounts that pursue both seed deals and traditional fund investments with smaller firms. Has 40% allocation for seed investments. Last deal was London-based Ledbury Capital, which began trading in July 2014.

## Pulse Capital

New York      *Start-up, Emerging*

Ibrahim Gharghour

212-430-1860, igharghour@pulsecp.com

Founded in 2011 by Investcorp alumni Ibrahim Gharghour, Gary Long and Thomas Middelhoff. Inked first deal in 2013 with statistical-arbitrage manager Sunofia Capital. Pulse was running just $22 million as of yearend 2014.

## Q Investments

Fort Worth, Texas    *Start-up*

Brandon Teague

817-332-9500, bteague@acmewidget.com

Since re-launching seeding business in 2010, has backed Gratia Capital of Los Angeles, North Yard Capital of New York and Spartan Capital of Charlotte. Primarily looks at long/short equity fund operators, but open to debt and event-driven strategies. Runs some $1.7 billion in a variety of vehicles. Almost half of capital supplied by partners.

## Reservoir Capital

New York    *Start-up*

Elizabeth Flisser Rosman

212-610-9000, erosman@reservoircap.com

Has begun talking to investors about assembling a second hedge fund-seeding vehicle. Debut vehicle now fully committed, pending the launch of Anil Prasad's Silver Ridge Asset Management, which has been delayed by a U.K. regulatory probe into currency trading at Prasad's previous employer, Citigroup. Fund 1 has backed managers including the 2015 launches of Abberton Capital, Castle Ridge Investment and OxBow Capital. Typically invests about $150 million per deal.

**RIT Capital**

London        *Start-up*

Ron Tabbouche

44-207-647-6203, investments@ritcap.co.uk

Publicly traded trust led by Jacob Rothschild has a £2.4 billion ($3.6 billion) market capitalization. Has seeded a number of Start-ups over the years in exchange for revenue shares. Most recent deal was this year's backing for Ed Eisler's macro fund. Backed Farmstead Capital in 2013 with a $100 million investment. Also backed Cresco Capital.



**SEB**

Stockholm     *Start-up, Emerging, Established*

Eric Hoh

46-85-062-3161, eric.hoh@seb.se

Swedish bank has made seed investments since 2003, and currently has about 20 positions. Takes equity stakes or enters revenue-sharing deals with both Start-ups and established managers pursuing liquid trading strategies. Last commingled seeding vehicle was the $300 million Manager Catalyst Fund 2, which is winding down. Now looking to deploy proprietary or client capital on a deal-by-deal basis to the tune of $10 million to $20 million per investment.

**Signet Capital Management Ltd**

London/Lausanne    *Start-up, Emerging*

Dr.Serge Umansky, CIO

44-207-968-4040, 41-21-620-464,
sumansky@signetmanagement.com

Long-established early backer of hedge funds, now owned by Mark Yusko's Morgan Creek. Signet has a special focus on fixed income solutions and market neutral investing.

**Stable Asset Management**

London       *Start-up, Emerging*

Erik Serrano Berntsen

44-207-016-3163 esb@stableam.com;

Tom Cheeseman

44-207-016-3166 tbc@stableam.com

Started 2009.The six firms seeded by Stable have raised a combined $3.7 billion.From Sept 2016 raising external capital for a pooled vehicle to back funds. Through new vehicle seeks to invest $50 million to $75 million apiece in 6-8 hedge fund-management firms in return for 20% shares of their revenue. It targets fund operators that follow niche, uncorrelated investment strategies with the potential to grow to $1 billion within their first few years.

## Strategic Capital Investors

London        *Emerging*

Mark Barker, founder and managing partner

44-207-340-8572, mbarker@stratci.com;

William Beverley, Head of Inv Risk & Quant Research

Accelerator fund part owned by Pacific Current Group. Has an initial commitment for up to $125 million from the £9.5 billion Common Fund of the Santander UK Group Pension Scheme. First placement was a three year $75 million investment with the John Street Systematic Fund managed by John Street Capital, London, established in 2012 by former Goldman Sachs and Winton Capital executives.

## Stride Capital

Stamford, Conn.     *Start-up, Emerging*

Don Rogers

203-569-8920, drogers@stridecapital.com

Since 2012, has backed four firms with initial investments of $25 million to $50 million each. Has been busy working with its managers to launch new products to complement their core offerings. Managers are Barnstar Funds, North Elm Capital, LRV Capital and Vertex Capital. Rogers formerly was a partner at SkyBridge Capital.

## Tages Capital

London        *Start-up, Emerging*

Mark De Klerk, Head of Seeding Strategies,

44-203-036-6051 mark.deklerk@tagesgroup.com;

Salvatore Cordaro, founding partner

salvatore.cordaro@tagesgroup.com

Claims to be Europe's largest seeder of hedge funds post Credit Crunch. Tages Group has a fund of hedge funds business and has offices in London and Milan. Average ticket size $50m for the equivalent of 20-30% of gross revenue. Recent deals - Anavon Global Equity and Dalton Asia Pacific.

## Tiger Management

New York    *Start-up, Emerging*

Fraser Seitel

201-784-8880, yusake@aol.com

Seeding legend has backed 30 Start-ups that now run a total of about $30 billion. Has stuck to its business model of investing about $20 million per deal, even as other seeders including Blackstone, Goldman Sachs and Reservoir Capital invest substantially more. Tiger largely operates as a family office for founder Julian Robertson. Only outside capital is in Tiger Accelerator Fund, which launched in 2011 with $450 million deployed to six Tiger seeds.

## Titan Advisors

Stamford, Conn.     *Start-up*

Nick Weisser

203-327-8600, nweisser@titanadvisors.com

Multi-manager operation with $5.5 billion overall is seeking to raise $400 million to $500 million for its first dedicated seed-capital vehicle. Plans to deploy $75 million to $100 million per deal. Previously backed Start-up Tide Point Capital in 2012.


## Witter Family Offices

New York     *Start-up*

Sherry Pryor Witter

212-753-7878, spryor@witterassets.com

Runs more than $500 million for descendants of brokerage legend Dean Witter, with 40% of the total in hedge funds, including seed investments. Began offering seed capital to fund Start-ups around 2011, and had backed at least 12 managers as of mid-2015. Targets boutique operations with investments of as little as $1 million.

# INDEX

262

263

265

## Q

## R

## S

OTHER BOOKS BY SIMON KERR

"Strategic Focus on European Hedge Funds" published by Informa
Business Publishing (1999, 248pp)

Printed in Great Britain
by Amazon